THE

GREEN MOUNTAIN

Travellers' Entertainment.

THE

GREEN MOUNTAIN

Travellers' Entertainment.

BY JOSIAH BARNES, Sen.,

NEW YORK:
DERBY & JACKSON, 498 BROADWAY.
1861.

W. H. Tinson, Stereotyper

Pudney & Russell, Printers

Preface.

A FEW preliminary words, dear reader, which you can run over in less than a minute.

There is one thing certain of writers: they cannot hide their imperfections. Defenseless individuals they are, and it would seem that they ought on that account alone to be charitably contemplated. Moreover they work for the gratification of their fellows—searching heaven and earth—often times the other place, too—for things which they may reduce to communicable shape. They wear out brain, muscle—turn night into day, and shed ink incalculably. All this they do with the fear of the Public constantly before their eyes, and with a nice regard to the Public's wants. Are they not *entitled* to charity? If they are not, I, as an humble, self-styled member of the fraternity, distinctly state, that I don't know why.

The book which you are now going to read (if according to Todd's advice you are reading the preface first) is just what it is—imperfect in many places, yet as a whole pretty much what I expected to make it. I started out with the intention of producing something that all those who read for amusement merely would find acceptable. I hope I have succeeded. I have worked hard enough for it, I know. I have worked earnestly, too. The characters which you will meet with have not been mere idle phantoms to me. I have laughed and I have wept with them. The thread of their lives has been mine. And they have not passed away. Oh, no! They live as really to my soul as the friend who sits beside me now.

But I will not tire you. I want you to begin fresh. And I want you to read right along, too. When you discover a fault, don't let your mind dwell upon it; for if you do, you'll miss the spirit of all that follows, make yourself sour, and pain me—if I should ever know it.

With my best wishes,

J. B., SEN.

Contents.

THE

GREEN MOUNTAIN

TRAVELLERS' ENTERTAINMENT.

INTRODUCTORY CHAPTER.

From an old memorandum book, lying in my drawer, I find that in the summer of 1836 I was travelling in the State of Vermont. My route lay to the northwest from Montpelier, through a sterile and thinly populated district. For want of a more expeditious and luxurious mode of conveyance, I was travelling on horseback.

The day had been fair and agreeable throughout; but as the sun drew near his setting, an ominous sign, in the shape of a long black cloud, loomed slowly from the western horizon. It grew larger as it arose—

blacker, broader, like a rising hemisphere, seemingly annihilating the golden sky in its course. The sun went down behind it, setting a resplendent diadem upon its great brow, which, however, soon faded, and the night came on gloomily. Red flashes from time to time lit up the rugged depths of that majestically rising cloud, and an oppressive stillness came down like the dew. Fascinated and absorbed with the imposing spectacle, which the playful lightnings revealed, I rode on leisurely, not noticing that the night had fully set in. A brighter flash, centered with a darting gleam, startled me from my reverie; and as the heavy thunder lumbered away with its fast-increasing train of echoes, I spurred my horse into a gallop.

An hour or so before, a pedestrian had informed me that I would find a public house about three miles ahead. Unhappily for me, my informant had chanced to be an honest Dutchman, lately arrived in the land of pumpkins and wooden condiments, and therefore spoke of miles in that transcendental sense which is the fashion of his country. This I was not aware of at the time, and had, with commendable sincerity, construed his answer to mean three English miles. Where is the public house? was my first thought, on getting my horse fairly into a gallop. Surely my three miles are up, I continued, seeing nothing in any direction that resembled a habitation of man. But the darkness limited my investigations, and I was left to push on along the narrow unfenced path, trusting for safety to my horse's sagacity, and to my own judgment, spasmodically enlightened by the fast-increasing flashes of lightning.

On I went at a rapid rate, calculating the distance I should be able to ride, after the rain should have seriously commenced, before my summer suit would cease to be protection against the torrent. On, on. The heavy voice of the angry storm coming to meet me, the pealing thunder, the quick gleams that lit up the rolling, tumbling, distracted mass overhead, suggested every moment the increasing necessity of shelter. Yet no shelter appeared. I reined my horse to a walk once, thinking that I saw a house; but the next flash proved it an illusion. Again, under full speed, I rushed along, leaving the superintendence of locomotion wholly to my horse, being absorbed myself in directing my vision most wistfully for some memento of man. But the livid lightning revealed nothing besides livid wastes of little hills and stony plains. At length my horse gave signs of fatigue, which I knew, from his mettle, had been concealed to the utmost, and would be followed by a general giving out. I had scarcely become conscious of this new feature in my dilemma, when the big, precursory drops began to fall. "Alas! it is inevitable," I said to myself, and, like a wise man, added, "let it come!" And it came—hail first, pelting remorselessly, thereafter a great flood, suffocatingly wet. I reined my horse to a disguised trot, which he voluntarily merged into a walk, and composed my inner man in accordance with the best philosophy I could summon at the moment. For a full hour I rode on. Still it rained—still no public house. My clothes and skin had almost, from the first dash, been so intimately connected, that they seemed equally parts of my body; and from my hands and feet, and all other possible extremities, ran steady streams of the liquid element. Human dignity had taken solemn flight, and human patience—even the very patient portion which I possessed—was about following, when the rain suddenly ceased, and the moon as suddenly came forth, revealing to me, among other things of less interest, the long-wished-for public house. It was hard by. A few minutes brought me to it, and a few more minutes found me with a dry suit on, and a dry yet fragrant cigar in my mouth. I sat down calmly by the capacious fire-place, and poking open the slumbering embers, I stroked the insides of my legs, and felt anxiety and ill-humor creeping up to my scalp, there to disappear in my hair, and comfort, like a full gush of sunshine, taking their place. I imbibed two or three draughts of soothing pleasure from my cigar, and looked around the room. It was a large one, and utterly devoid of even the semblance of ornament. The bare joists were smoked to perfection of brown, and the walls, which were of hewn logs, were of the same hue, modified and varied with occasional material accumulations from "man and beast." The fireplace was large enough to typify the "broad road" of psalmodic memory, and was made of stone without mortar. A row of benches—the homœopathic dilution of an architectural idea, ran along the four sides of the room, interrupted only by a square box in one corner, which reminded me of that box where men sometimes speak the truth. In the box was a lean, blear-eyed, long-nosed, long-haired, long-figured, on-the-whole-quite-unprepossessing young man. On two sides of him were ranged on four shelves about a score of bottles and decanters of various shapes and sizes. A big tumbler—bless the generosity of a by-gone age!—set upon the front edge of the box, which edge, for convenience, I suppose, was made about six inches wide. Over the young man's head hung a plain, heavy-looking gun, accompanied with a powder flask, which might have served for the horn of plenty. There were but two chairs in the room, both of which were as rigidly plain as an axe could make them. In one of those chairs I sat; and, after finishing my local survey, I again rubbed my legs, and felt bad humor travelling towards my hair, and fresh comfort warming me all over.

"Bad storm to-night," said I to the lean young man, my excess of comfort having overcome my pre-possession against him.

"I guess yew orter know," he responded, with a sort of starved grin.

"Many travellers lodge here to-night?" I hastened to inquire.

"Five 'r six 'r half a dozen, p'rhaps," he briefly answered, looking towards the outside door.

"Where are they?" I asked, with another flush of comfort; for I had experience enough in travelling to know that where half a dozen wayfaring men are met together, there is also the spirit of something not altogether barren.

"Perhaps yew'd like to see 'em," politely anticipated my box acquaintance.

"I would," said I, rising, and walking towards him.

"They're in the stoop out front," he began, coming out of his place, and walking, with great earnest strides, to the outside door. I followed.

"There," said he, pointing to the more distant end of the covered platform, and wheeling, strode back to his stronghold.

Left to introduce myself, I walked forward. I drew near unobserved, for two of the company were engaged in a discussion which fastened the attention of the rest. There were six of them. The first that attracted my attention was the one who was speaking at the moment. His dress was cut after the Quaker fashion, yet he was smoothly shaven and decently shorn, and his speech had all the elegant intonation and grammatical correctness of scholastic refinement.

I was strongly prepossessed in his favor at the first glance, for I clearly perceived, in his easy, elegant manner, a geniality, and a quiet, fascinating humor which indicated that he had learned the true lesson of life by heart, and bore it as an amulet about him. His antagonist in debate appeared to be a lawyer.

The tautology and mechanical arrangement of his speech, as well as his declamatory manner, indicated it. He was a stoutly built man, with thick, nicely turned side-whiskers, and a cut of lip that spoke of dignified resolution; and when I saw his heavy hand descend upon his stalwart thigh, to give emphasis to his suppressed tones, I fancied it might strike mortal blows where great things should be at stake.

Among the listeners was a rotund, floıid-faced, semi-centenarian. He appeared to be quite bald in the moonlight that night, with his hat off. There were deep crescent wrinkles in his cheeks and brow, which showed how natural it had always been for him to laugh, even at things too stale for other mèn. His eyes were large and staring, like a fish's; and as I looked at him, sitting there resting his chin upon the head of his cane, gazing intently at the disputants, his face bearing that stereotyped expression of jollity which seemed to mock the seriousness that had taken possession of him, I could not help but laugh a little in secret. By his side sat a small man, and a most singular phenomenon he was. He had the appearance of having been smoked and dried to the last degree consistent with physical life. His hair was dry and thin, as were also his garments. The skin of his face was most unreasonably and inextricably wrinkled, and his mouth and eyes were greatly sunken. But there was a fulness in his brow and a quickness in his eye that betokened something not manifested by the rest of his person. The remaining two were staunch farmer-like looking men, who had undoubtedly done good service to themselves, their families, and their country, yet were too modest to allude to it, or to anything else when there was an opportunity to listen.

Such were the "five 'r six, 'r half dozen" travellers whom my lean acquaintance had pointed out. After listening for a few minutes to the discussion, which from a serious political argument was passing rapidly to a mere play of words for the amusement of the listeners, I determined to advance and take an active part in the conversation, being somewhat addicted to political wrangling.

While debating within as to the appropriate manner of introducing myself, I became aware of the disagreeable shortness of my cigar. Not to be embarrassed by any unnecessary hindrance I plucked it from my mouth, and from a cursory view, seeing no more eligible direction, I squared myself to throw it over the heads of the parties disputing. I stood about ten feet from them, and not calculating the distance properly, I had the unspeakable mortification of seeing the fiery stub take its own course, which proved so wide from the one I had intended, that it struck with remarkable precision upon the nasal organ of the elegant Quaker. It was the work of but an instant to step forward, and most humbly and seriously apologize, for I was really very much mortified. He looked upon me with a good-natured smile, and said, "My friend, put a little more powder to your shot next time; shooting below the mark is a very common misfortune in this world," and wiping his soiled nose with great nicety, he put the whole affair into his pocket with his handkerchief.

"But," said I, "let me offer some slight atonement to you and to the company for the interruption I have caused to your entertainment. Will any or all of you step in and take a cigar—in con*dem*oration," I continued with an effort of pleasantry, "of the most uncivil deed just committed?" They responded unanimously in favor of my proposition, and we all went in and took peaceable possession of seven good cigars. By common consent we remained in the bar-room, and I became at once an accepted member of the company.

We all sat in silence for some minutes, each smoking and spitting after his own individual manner At length the silence, which was reaching quite an unpromising depth, was broken all to smash by the supposed lawyer's bursting out, "Well, gentlemen of —this—present company, what's to be done? This won't do. Here are six—seven cigars going like so many steam mills, and nothing but smoke being turned out, eh?"

"I suggest," piped in the little dry man, with a voice and manner that reminded me vividly of a choked hen—"I suggest that some one be appointed to tell a story."

"Then you hit it," responded the first speaker, emphatically. A general shifting of legs and discharge of saliva betokened the approval with which the suggestion was met by the rest.

"And, moreover," I ventured to add, "let us organize and proceed regularly to the appointment."

"Agreed!" closed in the lawyer. "Here I am, now, in this chair, president. Let's have the motion."

"But," —— commenced some one—

"Waiving all irregularities as to my getting my office," interrupted the lawyer, "let's have the motion."

Without further preliminary ado, a motion was made, seconded, and passed, to wit—that he, the president, be vested with the power of appointing the first one to attempt the proposed entertainment. Whereupon he said, "Well, let's see. The first, of course, will be a victim. I'll punish the suggestor. Sir!" addressing the dry man, "you I appoint, in virtue of my delegated power, to narrate a tale for the amusement of this present company. Proceed to your duty, and the Lord have mercy upon you."

We all laughed a little at the bombastic pleasantry of the president; and, when entire silence was restored, the dry man removed his cigar from his mouth, and, with a dignity and precision that surprised me, spoke in the substance of the following chapter.

CHAPTER II.

MR. PRESIDENT AND GENTLEMEN.—You require a hard thing of me. I am no story-teller. I am not social. I have not that gush of fellow-feeling which so warms the heart and makes brilliant the intellect. I have lost it all. Gone, gone with sunny days once mine. I am a gloomy man, yet I do not wish to communicate my gloom to you. Oh! far from it. I have suggested a thing here to-night, which I hoped might make the time pass more smoothly. I had no intention of taking a part, except as a listener. And now that I am forced to take the part which, by my consent, devolves upon me, I know not that I shall be able to forward the design I had in making the suggestion. I have no trivial tale to relate. I know none. There is but one story in my mind. It is the story of my life. If you will hear that, listen. I will be brief. I wish you could excuse me. Yet it will not be without a certain pleasure—a bitter, melancholy pleasure indeed, but still a pleasure—for me to tell you what has been my lot in this world.

I was an only child. I was born at sea, on board a vessel from Liverpool, bound for Calcutta. An old sailor, who made some pretensions to astrological erudition, remarked on deck, after hearing that a child had just come into the world in the cabin below, "God forbid! That child had better never been born. He will have a heavy sea to ride. Let them look well to his build." This my father told me many years after, as I bent to receive his dying blessing.

My father was at the time of my birth engaged in the East India trade. He had been peculiarly prosperous, and was the possessor of an immense fortune. Yet unsatisfied, he had again risked the dangers of the sea and a tropical climate, to add a few more thousands to his almost boundless wealth. My mother had always accompanied him in his voyages, choosing to risk her life rather than suffer the pangs of anxiety during his absence. I remember but little about her, for we were not long together. God grant that we may meet again! I might forget the past in her serene presence.

My childhood was pretty much like other childhoods, I suppose. Yet there are two incidents, very vivid in my memory, which happily do not always make a part of children's experience. The first which I shall relate was an adventure in which I most singularly escaped a horrible death.

My father was very fond of filling up his leisure with hunting. He was a daring man, and had the reputation of being the sharpest shot in all the region round about. He rode, on his hunting excursions, a powerful and well-trained horse, whose nimbleness, and almost human sagacity, had been of essential service to him in many a bloody and desperate encounter with that most ferocious and dreadful of wild beasts—the tiger.

I think I must have been about five years old, when one morning, as my father was preparing for his customary hunting excursion, I took it into my head to accompany him. I accordingly laid my wish before him, and was astonished to find that he would not hear to it at all. I pressed into service every means of persuasion I could muster, but he only patted my head, and told me to go to my mother now, and I should hunt when I should get to be a big man like himself. This did not satisfy me, and I went away grumbling, and determined to go anyhow. I watched the direction they took, and arming myself with a toy spring-gun I set out after them. I was soon out of sight of my father's house, toiling on with great imaginary bravery along the beaten track worn by the hunters in their frequent excursions from town. As I was strutting along, entirely impregnable to the idea that I might get lost, I came to a narrow path leading off from the main track, which had such a cool, leafy, romantic appearance that I took it, and pursued its course for perhaps an hour, when it suddenly ended in a dark pool to which not a bit of sunshine penetrated. For the first time I began to feel uneasy. I began to think about my mother and home, and continued to think about them until I was overcome with the feeling, and cried heartily. Crying relieved me and made me brave again, and I took up the spring-gun, which I had thrown down in my incipient despair, — determined to make my way back to the main track. I went on very vigorously for some time, growing very impatient at the seemingly interminable length of the narrow, crooked path before me. Finally I became sensible of fatigue. It gained rapidly upon me, and soon my aching limbs gave out entirely, and I sank down by a thick growth of underbrush, my head swimming and my eyes pierced with keen pains. The exquisite gratification sitting down gave me made me think for a while I would never get up again.

I sat there some considerable time, and, at last being rested, I began again to think of my home, and with the thought came an awful sense of fear. Cold sweat started out all over me. I jumped up and seized my little gun, but quickly dropped it, for I felt something cold and slimy contract suddenly in my hand. Fortunate it was that instinct served me so promptly and faithfully, for a viper of the most deadly character shot away through the dead leaves like an arrow. I had grasped it in my hand! I again picked up my gun and trudged on—this time with no notion whatever which direction I was taking, and with no purpose except to get along—a vague idea that I should get home before dark being the only thought of my mind. How long, how very long was that afternoon! As I toiled on a kind of insensibility came over me. I neither cried nor felt afraid; and I really began to feel that the woods were not so very bad a place after all. Towards sunset, as I sat by a large decaying log, busied with plucking some tiny flowers for my mother, who I knew was very fond of them, I felt myself suddenly seized by some irresistible power and borne away through the thicket with a wild rush which so bewildered me that I could not stir a limb. I had never seen a tiger alive, but I instinctively felt I was in the jaws of one. Fortunately my clothes held the weight of my body, for his keen teeth had only seized on them. Had my clothes given way the second hold would have been more secure! I had just recovered from the first shock sufficiently to be fully conscious of my situation, when I felt a stinging sensation in my head, and I remember no more until I found myself in the arms of my father. I heard him relate the circumstance of my rescue to my mother that night. The party was returning from an unsuccessful hunt, my father being about a hundred yards in advance. Coming out of a jungle he saw a huge tiger with something in its mouth, stealing along the opposite side of the glade upon which he had just entered. His horse saw it at the same instant, and started off unbidden in full pursuit. The action of the horse surprised my father, for it was a part of its training never to commence pursuit voluntarily. From the nature of the ground my father was aware that pursuit would be not only fruitless but dangerous; and, after permitting the caprice for a few moments, he attempted to rein in the horse for the purpose of rejoining the company. To his surprise he found himself unable to do it. The horse seemed in a frenzy—so fierce was its eagerness to overtake the wild beast.

After two or three unsuccessful attempts to stop or divert the horse, which, though at an alarming speed, did not gain upon the tiger, my father gave a sign for the company to follow, and yielded himself to the direction of his horse. A few moments more and the tiger turned to cross the glade, which was long and narrow. It was in fair view. It was the only chance, for the tiger was evidently making for the thicket, which at that time of day would effectually shield it from further pursuit. Though at an unusual distance he determined to have a shot. Utterly unconscious of the to him infinite importance of that shot, he fired carelessly; but some good angel had touched his nerves, and the bullet pierced the heart of the bounding tiger. It gave a tremendous leap in the air, and fell dead. "Thanks to the noble horse!" said my father. He would not say it now!

The second incident that varied the monotony of my childhood, was the death of my very dear mother. With her sunk a star which might have led me to another destiny. She died a few days before the anticipated final departure of us all to England. Her illness was short, and her death quite unexpected, as I have often heard my father say. I remember, with the utmost distinctness, though but in my sixth year, how she looked when clothed for the grave, and how my father wept, standing beside her. I had never before seen my father weep, and it was a terrible sight to me. I remember asking him why he talked to my poor mother, as I called her, who was dead, and could not hear him; and I wondered why he took me up when I said that, and hugged me so long. But I understand all those things now; how clearly my story will show.

Soon after my mother's death, my father, with me, embarked for England, where we arrived, after a prosperous voyage. I was directly placed under the grim supervision of a teacher of Greek and Latin, and urged through the usual course preparatory to the acquiring of my vernacular. Solemn days grew into solemn weeks; and the latter built up months—tedious months from which came years—two long years, of which I have but a cloudy remembrance, relieved by occasional beams of sunshine, when I was permitted to go with my father, who seemed to have no control over me, into the country, to spend a week after the manner of joyous childhood. At the end of the two years I was placed under another teacher, who was more mild and genial, and who improved upon the soil, so manured and harrowed by the former husbandman of young mind, by sowing therein seeds of more practical knowledge. With him I acquired considerable proficiency in reading, writing, and speaking, according to rule, my mother tongue. I remained with him, off and on, a long time—seven years, I think, and left his roof to enter upon the treadmill course of "collegiate education." Being of an active turn, and quick to imbibe, I soon attracted considerable attention in that palace of words and diagrams, called Oxford University; but it was short-lived. I soon tired of committing Latin paragraphs and Greek stanzas, and exhibiting my skill in mathematics, by elaborately-solved geometrical problems; and, at the advice of a vocalist of considerable note, devoted myself more particularly to the cultivation of a talent for music, which, from early childhood, I had manifested to a somewhat remarkable degree. I gave up my college studies altogether, and, at the age of eighteen, commenced my real career. My natural gift was not long developing under the excellent tuition which my father's wealth brought me. At the age of twenty I gave my first concert, which was received with enthusiastic applause, and introduced me at once to the world as a gifted vocalist. My youth added furor to the public sentiment regarding me, and in a few months I found myself the burdened object of universal admiration, as far as I knew. These were happy days. Bright, indeed, do they appear to me now, far over the dismal desert. I have now a circumstance to relate, which was the subtle starting point of all my woes. And let me premise, that if, in what follows, I exhibit the reflection of the heart-tearing agonies I have endured, it shall not be imputed to me as weakness to be despised, but be charitably contemplated.

It was on a moonlight evening. I was returning from a concert, where my efforts had been received with unusual applause, and, flushed with the glory of success, was passing a residence of splendid exterior, when my eye was caught with an angelically beautiful face, turned towards the slightly waned moon, smiling down from midheavens. The owner of that face was leaning over a low gate; and as she stood there, looking far off into the serene sky, so divinely beautiful did she appear, that I involuntarily stopped to gaze at her, I stood but a moment, and then passed on; yet the image remained in my mind, gradually deepening into my heart. From that moment, I was in love; and it was my first love, deep, pure, and as earnest as life.

The town where this happened, was a place of but temporary sojourn to me; and though I had no intimate acquaintance there to whom I could confide my desire for an introduction, I yet determined to have an interview with the object upon which my imagination had taken so strong a hold. Owing to the difficulty I have mentioned, it was several weeks before it was brought about. But I triumphed over all hindrances; and one balmy afternoon, I was decently and auspiciously presented to the young lady, whom I shall call Emily, for convenience. Unlike some moonlight scenes, I found daylight gave additional charm. My imagination had, meanwhile, been very liberal, but I was not long in discovering that it had not even done justice to her. I was literally entranced with the exquisite grace and tenderness of her manner. Her exterior entirely displaced my beau ideal of female beauty; and when, on passing from the introductory common-places of conver sation to more solid talk, I found her sensible and thoughtful, and withal witty, you may well conclude that a general displacement came to pass within me. I was intoxicated with the ambrosial draught. It inspired me, and I discoursed enthusiastically. Finally, at the suggestion of the friend who had introduced me, I sang; I sang a ballad which had a mournful ending; and as I dwelt with deep feeling upon the last refrain, I saw the pearly tears chase each other down her cheeks, pale with emotion.—Oh! that was a happy moment to me—unutterably happy. Heaven alone can give me such another. I departed glowingly from her presence, and withdrew myself from the companionship of the friend who was with me, retiring along the unfrequented shores of a creek in the vicinity, to think over the things of the afternoon. The gushing happiness that had at first overwhelmed me, passed on like any other momentary tide, and left me in a speculative mood. It was my song, and not I, that had moved her so deeply. I remembered of having seen large auditories in tears, at the same ballad, before. "I have made no especial impression; and yet"—— In this line I speculated until the tolling of a distant clock admonished me of the lateness of the hour, loth to arrive at any conclusion, because the right one could not be arrived at from the premises. But on my way home, I came to a wholesome determination, which was, to lay siege, which, if needs be, I would turn into a blockade, and patiently await the result. I began to execute my plan of operation, by making it convenient to pass the house of my beloved two or three times a day, looking up the third time of passing each day. I generally saw her at the window above, set in flowing crimson, and lace curtains, like a painted picture. One day, I caught a smile of recognition from her, which encouraged me—I was grown wondrous bashful—to call upon her. The interview was long and undisturbed; yet I made but a poor figure, being very dull, actually sleepy, though it was in the afternoon, and uncontrollably absent-minded. But I was far from insensible. That dear image went deeper into my heart at every gaze. Her manner towards me was so artless, so unreserved, that I ventured to repeat my visit after a short interval. The reception I met with was ever so cordial, so vivifying, that I soon ceased to draw pleasure from anything else. My profession was forgotten, my reputation, my friends, everything but the sweet, ever-thought-of Emily. I wanted her to know how I felt. I became exceedingly impatient to dissolve before her, and beseech her to love me, as I loved her. But I was proud, and feared a repulse. She was ever friendly to me, yet nothing more, so far as I could see. I knew she was fond of my society, loved to hear me sing, respected my taste, studied to please me. But this knowledge gave me no satisfaction. At length, I became after a manner desperate, and rushed headlong to a fierce determination, namely, that I would tell her just how I felt, frankly, and ask her frankly what was to be done. This

I did with many sighs, and some tears; and was encouraged to hope by her remaining silent the while. When the scene was over, she took my hand, and playfully diverted me with fancyings oddly timed yet like her—of how the villages in America looked, and the cottages, and the great forests, the lakes, the solitary streams, the quiet, uninhabited valleys of which she had read, talking on so sweetly for an hour. Strange girl! thought I, as I walked home, so cool, and still so bewitching. A shadow fleeted across my soul that night. It was the first dim moving of the dreadful storm, whose fruit was to waste my life.

So much time had been squandered in pursuit of this sole object of my then existence, that its accumulated length now attracted my attention; and I felt a dawning conviction of the necessity of changing my social habits a little. Having relieved myself of a portion of the burden, I found it not at all disagreeable to accept the next invitation to attend a select party. It was at the house of a stranger, and my attendance was, I might say, professional. I was highly gratified with the proceedings of the evening, until near the close, when, after having sung to the overwhelming satisfaction of the company, I heard some one ask another member of the party if he also would furnish a song. It seemed to me a little out of taste, but I joined the rest in pressing the invitation. The invited, after much urging, took a seat at the piano. He was young and strikingly handsome, having a noble expression of countenance, and modest demeanor. I had never seen him before, and had not noticed him particularly that evening. With subdued touch his fingers ran over the shining keys, and in a moment I felt that he was a master. In the trembling chimes of the dying prelude his voice came gently into harmony, and waved off into a gushing melody so sweet and unaffected, yet so skillful,—again I felt he was a master. He sang one song, and then retired, leaving the room. "Who is he?" asked a lady near me. His name was given. No one of the party had ever heard it before, except the informer.

The next day I saw an announcement, plentifully placarded upon the fences and lamp-posts, signifying that a Mr. S—— would favor the public with some choice vocal efforts that evening. He is to be my rival, eh? I reflected with a tinge of bitterness, for I knew his power, I had felt it the night previous.

I determined to go and hear him. To stay away, I wisely thought, would be accounted jealousy. And I will take Emily, too, I further resolved, and she shall thereby know the nobleness of my disposition. At the appointed hour for the concert, I called upon Emily for the purpose of carrying the latter resolution into effect, when, to my great discomfiture, I found her just at the point of starting in the company of the young vocalist himself. The incident was as unexplainable as unexpected to me, and embarrassed me very much. Yet I behaved myself as well as I knew how; and she was *so* friendly, *so* sincerely regretted the circumstance that was to deprive her of my society for the evening, that I was somewhat reinstated, and went home quite calm, forgetting, however, that I ought to have been at the concert, until it was quite too late. The next day the whole city was vocal with praises of the brilliant Mr. S——, which, of course, grated roughly upon my ear. Not so much because his sudden splendor bedimmed mine in the eyes of the public, but because of its connection with my Emily. And the dismal uncertainty I labored under regarding her feelings towards me did not help the matter. I thirsted for an explanation. That evening I visited Emily and obtained it.

"You were previously acquainted with him?" I remarked.

"Oh, no," she replied, "he is the son of a friend of my father. No, I never saw him until last night."

This was great relief. My chance is as fair as his, then, at any rate, I thought; and we'll see.

A letter from my father, urging me to come and see him, had been lying in my drawer for several days unanswered. I had taken it out that morning for the purpose of answering it, telling him I could not come. Some trivial incident had diverted me from it for the moment, and I had placed it in my pocket, and forgotten it. On pulling my handkerchief out of my pocket to mollify a sneeze, just after Emily had uttered her explanation, I drew with it the letter. It fell upon the floor before her, and she picked it up. "Read it," said I. "It is from the best of fathers, to, I fear, an ungrateful son."

"Why don't you go?" she remarked on finishing it. I blunderingly hinted at the true reason, and asked her what she would do under like circumstances.

"Go, indeed I should. Your father is the best friend you have on earth." I groaned, and spoke of something else; yet inwardly determined to go.

Accordingly I went. I was absent several weeks, undergoing, meantime, all sorts of tortures. Being far distant from her, I could reflect more coolly. I brought in review all that had transpired, and was often near the conviction that I had acted very foolishly, and that it was a mere wild-goose chase to attempt to arouse any passion in her. So near was I to this conviction, that I believe I should have ultimately taken an oath never to return—O! that I had taken such an oath!—had not my father, after hearing an enthusiastic description of the place from me, proposed making it his permanent residence. I encouraged the proposition; and he accordingly disposed of his mansion in London, where he was then living, and we together set out, he to visit, and I to return to, the city of my hopes and discontent.

As I was sitting in my room the morning after our arrival at the point of destination, moodily reflecting, I experienced a sudden enlightenment from the idea, that probably my fears of rivalship, which had grown to be quite formidable, were mere moonshine.

His escorting her to the concert was merely an act of gallantry in itself; and I had no reason to suppose that it must necessarily be followed by further amatory advances. It was a happy thought, and comforted me marvellously. I whistled "God save the King!" and cut a dancer's flourish, in which I tore my coat, and expressed my satisfaction in two or three other silly ways, being alone; and then, in a most happy mood, went down stairs for the purpose of going out to call on my old acquaintances. Just as I reached the outside door, my eyes were filled with an object which completely astounded me. All my fears came darkly back and took me captive again. My confusion and abasement were indeed quite overwhelming, for the object was none other than Emily, my adored, rosy and sparkling, with Mr. S——, smiling and excited, in a superb carriage passing at a glorious rate. "Perhaps they are going now on their wedding trip, who knows?" said I bitterly to myself, willing to magnify my misery. I gazed after them, feeling that shadow again sweep chillingly over my soul. It had not yet reached to a thought—dread parent of the deed!

A week passed before I called on Emily: and

almost the first thing she said to me, was to rehearse the pleasures of that ride, the commencement of which I had witnessed. This she did so ingenuously, and so regretted my not having been with them, that I felt ashamed of my silly suspicion, and of the sentiment that accompanied it. She also expressed exceeding satisfaction at the determination of my father, "which," said she, looking tenderly into my face, "will, I am sure, secure me the society of *one* devoted friend at least." If I had not known her as well as I did, I should have taken this remark as an insult. But I was fully aware that she spoke from her inmost heart, and it only made me love her the more.

My father succeeded in purchasing a mansion suited to his wishes, and we took possession of it, my father and myself, living alone, our household affairs being regulated by an aunt of mine, who had to the age of forty lived without having excited the serious desires of the stronger sex. Having a home again, and its new attachments, I prosecuted my siege more leisurely, yet also more seriously. After the lapse of two or three months, my impatience overcame me again, and I repeated my ardent declaration. This time my importunity—I was really desperate—overcame her patience, and she frankly told me, that I was too impetuous; that she did not want to hear me talk so. "When, then, O, angel!" I exclaimed, insanely fervent, "shall I have a period to my woes?" She made no reply, and I went on. "How shall I teach you to love me? Can I make *any* sacrifice? Will my life serve you? take it. It is no longer mine, but thine, my dearest Emily. *Can* you give me hope?" To this, and much more like unto it, she said nothing. Suspicion crept into my excited soul, and I gave it voice. "Would you be mine were it not for another?" She made no reply. She was weeping. I interpreted her emotion my own way. "She loves another, but will not make me an enemy," I said deep in my heart; and with it was born a deadly hatred towards my long-dreaded rival. I went from her presence fiercely determined never to see her again.

For several days I underwent the dreadful struggle between passion and pride; and I began to fear the former would conquer, whereupon I concluded to make a journey to the Continent. I believe my sainted mother from on high gave me that impulse; but the machinations of hell prevailed.

Who started the idea I know not; but in the

midst of my preparations for departure, I was surprised with a visit from a man, who introduced himself as a committee of one, authorized to invite me, in the name of the town, to enter the lists for a strife of musical powers, the proceeds of the entertainment to be given to the poor. The idea pleased me; but who was to be my competitor? He politely informed me that Mr. S—— had consented to sustain that relation to me. The hated obstacle to my happiness! But I would not shrink. I was confident I could overshadow him. I signified my approval of the plan, and my acceptance of the invitation, and consequently deferred my setting out on the anticipated journey for the time being.

Still the struggle within me continued. It took away my ambition, and impaired my voice. To such an extent did it thus operate on me, that I was at the point of withdrawing myself from the anticipated musical strife altogether, when the following singular circumstance transpired.

Some time had elapsed since my last interview with Emily, and I had pretty well settled into the conviction that she was quite indifferent to me, and my consuming passion. One close of day, as I was sitting by the window, watching the fading of the glorious autumnal twilight, a little boy was announced. I called him to my side, and he gave me a letter. I did not know the hand-writing of the superscription, but opened it with trembling haste, suspecting who the author was. Glancing at the end, I saw it was from the cruel Emily. Yet, the letter did not surprise me, as did the contents thereof. I read it twice, and reflected upon it some time, before I could rest satisfied it was not all a dream. The letter was as follows; I can repeat it word for word--

"MY VERY DEAR FRIEND:—I know you are unhappy. I know you are offended with me. If you knew my heart, you would believe me when I say, you are angry without a cause. They tell me I am a strange being. Perhaps I am. They tell me I am incapable of the passion of love. Perhaps I am. It is true, I have often wished I could have been so made, that I could have the friendship without the love of men. I know not what to do. I have no objections to marrying; but I must not make an enemy by it. Mr. S—— has made a declaration similar to that which you have twice made. What shall I do? I prize you both very highly. I cannot marry either of you at the expense of the other's friendship. A happy suggestion came to my mind to-day. The papers announce that you are to test your musical capacities in a friendly strife. The one who succeeds may appropriate me as his trophy. Will you consent to it? Can you consent to it, and remain friendly if disappointed? I know well that you both love me very much. I hope I am worthy of your loves. They tell me disappointed lovers are the worst of enemies. Do you believe it? Can you, if the issue should be against you, set an example to the contrary? I am unhappy. I wish you would consent to this. If you triumph, I will be your wife; if you fail, I will yet be your friend.

EMILY.

"P. S. I have sent a duplicate of this to Mr. S."

Oh, how ardently did I consent to this arrangement! I knew the prize would be mine, and that my thorny pilgrimage would be crowned with a triumphant entry into the paradise of all my earthly hopes. I briefly acquainted Emily with my acquiescence in what she proposed; and set about preparing myself for the trial, the issue of which was to be of such vital importance to me.

Great excitement prevailed in the city. From our known talents, and the stimulus the occasion would afford, the music-loving confidently anticipated a glorious treat.

At length, the day closed that was to usher in the night of—my destiny. We were to sing alternately, occupying three hours in all; the decision to be passed by a committee, appointed for that purpose.

At the time announced for the beginning, I

entered the crowded hall; and as the cheers of the expectant throng died away, I felt as though I would risk my life upon the result, so confident was I of success. My competitor was already there; and as I turned to take a seat upon the stage, I caught a glimpse of the fair enchantress, far back in the dense multitude. That inspired me anew. I was impatient to begin. The singing commenced,—my rival opening the performance. He sang a beautiful song, about the coming of some happy day, when heaven would descend to earth, and all should feel the flow of praise and adoration welling in the heart, a living, eternal tide of tearless beatitude; and as he wandered among the mazes of the intricate, yet rapturous melody, I could not help but be conscious of a new tone in his young voice—a development which I had not looked for, and which annoyed me very much.

I saw the audience sway with his growing energy. And when the last sweet trill melted away like an embodied sound, floating far into the deep, limitless sky, and I saw the rapt listeners pale with exquisite pleasure, my heart for a moment sank within me. I followed him, and sang as I had never sung before; and though I was enthusiastically applauded, I could plainly see that I failed to produce that deep effect which accompanied my antagonist's effort. He sang again. Again he sat down without cheers, so rapt was the audience. My second attempt was more successful; but I had what seemed an Orpheus to contend with. I became desperate. Having the closing song, I chose the ballad which I had sung at my first interview with Emily. The closing verses spoke the real feeling of my intensely agitated heart. They were the words of a lover, in utter despair. I gave entirely away to the tide of feeling, and had the satisfaction of producing that voiceless effect, which I desired. But it was a poor satisfaction. I knew very well that my rival had on the whole, triumphed; and I passed a sleepless night, harrowed with terrible presentiments. In the morning, I was waited upon by a delegate from the committee, and presented with a sealed note, without remarks. I knew its contents; I needed not to read them. I seized my hat, and went forth beneath the smile of that serene autumnal morning, cursing my God, and wishing I could die. Life from a spread of flowers, and tuneful groves, bounded with a horizon of warm beauty, was suddenly, like a change in a dream, transformed into a bleak, rock-bound, fog-mantled dungeon, without hope.

I strolled along the creek, where I had wandered the spring before, venting the pent agony of my spirit in groans and lamentations. The first gush of tearful emotion past, the sickening thought, that another was soon to enjoy what I had so lately looked upon as mine, took possession of me, and with it *that shadow*, like the first wave of insanity. Murder was in my heart. If it had been merely in regard to Emily, that he had succeeded, I think honor would have deterred me from interfering; but he had, innocently, to be sure, yet that I did not consider, cast a shade upon my reputation as a singer. It stung like a viper, and I believe clenched my shadowy purpose. "He shall not enjoy her," I said aloud, and smote the air. I afterwards thought, as my mind coldly settled upon a plan, "I shall but die of my most cruel disappointment. If justice find me out, and I perish, it will be but a coveted period to a life surcharged with woes." Miserable, short-sighted youth! how little didst thou count the cost of thy insane purpose! The only consolation, or palliation there is, is that I did not work alone. The fiends of deepest hell were my abettors.

My unsuspecting victim left town that morning, so I was informed on my return, to visit his mother—he was a widow's son—a short distance away, intending to return in the evening. That I might not be suspected, I made a show of illness to two or three of my young friends, and went home early in the evening, ostensibly to retire to bed. Arrived at home, I provided myself with an excellent pistol, which I had owned for some time, and was perfectly accustomed to, and went forth on my bloody mission. I took a round-about way, and reached the road by which I knew he must return, about three miles from the city limits. It was a solitary place. The road skirted a huge precipitous rock, for about a quarter of a mile. On the side opposite the upper rock, was another precipice of considerable depth, up which came the murmur of a foaming stream below. Here, in the shadow of the rock, I posted myself. The night was clear and windy. It was a mournful wind, and might have prophesied to me, had I listened. But conscience was stifled in the raging of the fiendish passions within. I heard only the sounds of hissing scorn from the world, at my late failure, and the sounds of amatory endearment between the angel captor of my soul, and another. I grated my teeth, and clenched the cold, passive instrument of death. I heard the sound of horse's hoofs. I knew that S—— had gone out on horseback. The terrible excitement under which I labored, sharpened every sense, and I felt that it was he. I threw off my cloak, and placed my right elbow upon a projection of the rock, that my aim might be sure. My position was hardly assumed when he came in sight, his horse galloping leisurely. On he came, so near that I clearly recognized him. The horses ears were pointed towards me. "Now is the time," I fiercely whispered, for conscience pulled hard at my arm, and—O, my God! I tell it not willingly—discharged the deadly weapon. The horse stopped suddenly still; the rider bent low over its neck, clinging by the mane. The shot was fatal. I saw him fall heavily to the ground. The spell was broken. The enormity of the deed glared at me like a wandering spectre. I hurriedly left the spot, getting home, I hardly knew how. I entered my room, and locked the door, and sat down to reflect upon what I had done. But I could not reflect. I could not remain in my chair; I could only walk the floor beating my breast in the agony of remorse. As I walked, I felt a death-like chill creeping along my nerves. I looked at my hands; they were blue and stiff like a corpse's. The lamp, and then the windows multipled; the walls danced and whirled; the floor rose beneath me; a dark rush, like diving into deep, still water, and I was lost to consciousness of external things. I came back to this world amidst the smell of drugs, and the close, heavy air of a sick-room. I had been very ill several days,—delirious, they told me, raving almost continually. Had I disclosed the awful secret? How could I know. I told my nurse that I had had a painful dream of killing a man; and asked her if I had done injury to any one. She assured me to the contrary, and bade me be quiet. Being stronger the next day, my father came in to see me; gravely and feelingly he told me of the diabolical murder that had been committed; his words were keen arrows shot unerringly through my heart. With remarkable self-possession, I asked him some questions concerning it, and the matter passed by.

As day by day I arose from my prostration, I felt the communion with my past life severed, and the gory deed with which my hands were imbrued coming out in dark relief, a haunting, avenging shape.

Many weeks crept monotonously away before I could again go forth into the sunshine and the fields; and when I did, the former was but a mockery, and the latter white with the mantle of winter. Like my heart were all things; but unlike that they had the embryo of spring. The undying worm within fed upon my returning vitality, and my recovery was slow, and sometimes doubtful. It was agreed to, among my physicians, that a sojourn in some milder climate would be beneficial to me. Accordingly I renewed my preparations for a journey to the Continent. My destination was Naples, whereat in due time, and without accident, I arrived. Here was a new world for me. Diverted by the multitude of new and interesting objects that surrounded me, I rapidly regained my health, and even my old buoyancy of spirits. My voice returned; and intoxicated with the applause it brought me, and being surrounded with all that could fascinate, I gradually lost sight of the demon that pursued me.— I forgot that I was a murderer.

I remained in Naples three years. At last its pleasures became stale to me, and I longed for home. Having no other guide than inclination, I obeyed it, and went back to England. My father had grown old very much. He wept, and embraced me; which I was pained to behold, for in him it was an indication of dotage. The extraordinary activity and privation of his early life had prematurely exhausted the fountain, and now grey, bent, and emaciated, he was tottering rapidly to the grave. The hope of meeting and embracing me once more had for months supported him. Now that his wish was gratified, he sank soon, and was no more. He died blessing his only son, and calling upon God to grant him a long life of usefulness and happiness.

I was an orphan. My new sorrow for a time hindered the return of remorse. But it was soon brought back with redoubled fury by learning that an innocent man had, in my absence, been arrested and executed for the deed of which I alone was guilty. Oh! the tearless, scathing agony that burnt deep into my writhing heart! Yet there was no help. Pardon from on High I could not ask, and men knew not my guilt, knew not my wretchedness, to forgive or to sympathize. I was alone, Oh! how dismally alone!

Why it was I have never been able to explain; but true it is, that from the horrid depth into which I had fallen I looked to Emily. I loved her then. Oh! I had never ceased to love her. Could she be mine, I thought; and could we together go to some place remote from this, where things around could no more speak to my heart of its hellish crime, I would yet be happy and willing to live.

I wrote to her: yes, this bloody right hand that had deprived her of a noble and devoted husband wrote to her, asking her to be mine. Many days I feverishly awaited a reply. It came, a barbed flaming dart. It was but one line, firmly written,

"I cannot be the wife of a murderer." She knew my secret, and had kept it. Could I have loved an angel from Heaven more? Could I have feared more the arm of Omnipotent Justice?

Thus was the last hope crushed, the last tie that bound me to the land of my fathers severed. She who had been the innocent cause of my wasting, undying misery, who had once shone so warmly into my soul, had withdrawn herself far from me for ever. She was to be thenceforth as a star mirrored upon my turbulent soul, a cold, scattered brightness.

I became a voluntary exile. I went to Germany. There the new climate, and novel circumstances, like the fascinations of Naples, soothed me for a time, and I began again to hope. I strove to forget entirely my past life. And that I might succeed, I adopted the language and customs of the country. For five years I neither read, spoke, nor thought an English word voluntarily. At the end of that time, I had made such progress in my new way of life, that I was able to mingle freely in society. My talents as a vocalist shone out brilliantly again; and they, coupled with my great wealth, gave me high standing. Still the bloody deed haunted me, coming out more bold as things became familiar around me. I thought again of wandering. But a new attraction appeared. A young countess, a widow, beautiful, and adorned with all the graces that art could bestow, and of a disposition mild and melancholy, tender and loving, became a member of the Society to the entertainment of which I often contributed. She too was a singer; and in the mazy realm of music we approached one another. I loved her: not as I first loved—as purely, but not so rapturously. My soul seized upon her as one drowning seizes the tendered object of salvation. In her was passion deep as the sea. Her marriage had been one of convenience; and she had never loved before. She gave herself to me, and we were married. In her loving embrace I again ceased to feel for a fleeting period that I was a murderer. Life again opened before me a shining vista; and I could look back with a feeling akin to defiance. The clear moon told a new tale; the mournful winds lost their burden, their moaning rehearsal of that fatal night, and took the tone which had charmed my spirit in childhood. Time cast off his chains, and took the soft, swift pinions of the dove; weeks became as days, and days as hours. I was happy; yet not completely happy. There was a dread, like the heavy sound of a distant storm at sea,—deep, underlying all—a dread of the future.

The anniversary of our nuptials was made glad with the birth of a child—a daughter. This circumstance weaned me yet more from my past life,—dimmed yet more the hideous remembrance.

Another year bore me smoothly and rapidly on. My little girl, now a sweet blue-eyed prattler, could call me father. Father! Why did it so affect me? I well remember the thrill of agony that sacred word first from her smiling lips sent through my soul. I withdrew the hand which would have patted her ruddy cheek—that hand was stained with a brother's blood! I gasped and trembled with the depth of my emotion; and the little cherub ran frightened from me.

But it was not long so. It was but a passing throe of dormant conscience.

Another year was added to my illusive dream.

One day my little treasure climbed to my knee, and told me her mother was sick. I started as one struck by the assassin's blade. Directly a domestic came in and confirmed the artless utterance of the little lisper. In a moment I was at her side. She was really very ill. She had been suddenly attacked with a malignant and fatal epidemic with which the city was then being scourged, and from a knowledge of her constitution I knew she must die. I sent for a physician, who gravely confirmed my awful conviction—awful! for what had she not been to me? to what was I now to awake?' "Can you not save her?" I wailed beseechingly. The kind and sympathizing physician pointed with tears to the mark of death. There was no hope. I felt its feeble glimmer perish within me, and overwhelmed I sank in a long, deep swoon.

As I came out of the rayless void, a grim spirit seemed to whisper in my ear, "The murderer has dreamed his dream of bliss. Henceforth, shall be toiling among lacerating rocks, and blinding lightnings, until the great gulf of destruction swallow him up for ever!" I resisted the kind efforts that would restore me to this world, and longed to die. Life was worse than worthless to me. I stood as one might stand upon the skirts of a limitless desert, while vengeful furies urged on behind to lash him with their serpent scourges forward for ever upon the arid waste. When they told me she was dead, my mind refused the guidance of my will, and I howled like a frightened maniac.

In a few hours nature so far prevailed over the tortures of my spirit, that I was sufficiently recovered to visit the chamber of death.

I stood by her dead body, and took up my child. It was then I thought of my own childhood; of the story of my birth, and what the sailor said; of the tiger, and cursed the ball that saved my life; of how my mother died, and my father wept, pressing me to his heavy heart; and as my mind dwelt tenderly on that, tears came to my burning eyes, and I wept long and freely.

A few dismal days passed dimly on, and she was buried. When the always sad—to me trebly—mournful ceremony was over, I returned to my desolated home firmly resolved upon self-destruction. But when I saw my child, and felt the beams of her sunny soul, my will swerved, and I put away for the time the dark resolve. But that frail support to my sinking spirit was not spared me long. Ere the grass grew upon the grave of the mother, the lonely—wandering little innocent was laid by her side.

Again utterly alone, I would have persevered in my former purpose. But I had grown thoughtful, and shrank from passing that bourn whence there can be no return. I sought relief from intoxicating drinks. I drank deeply. From drinking I fell to gambling, and my wealth soon melted away, leaving me in a few months penniless. My position in society lost, I mingled with outcasts the most forlorn of all, and walked familiarly with villains, yet not myself a villain. No; the one great crime that had thrust me into this terrible abyss, had been the rash deed of unthinking youth. I could not commit another. The awful remembrance debarred me.

At first the stimulating draught had quieted me; but now it ceased to befriend. The avenging shape kept pace with every pulsation of my weary heart, stabbing without mercy. It mingled with the ravings of my drunkenness, and glared hotly upon me in the silent hours of solitude.

Lower, and lower I sank, until all men spurned me, and I went aside like a wounded brute to die. I lay in an open hovel. It was a cold winter night. I lay upon the bare, frozen earth, and waved my hand in the keen air, and blessed it for the numbing frosts it bore to freeze my blood, so earnest was my longing for death—for a period to my innumerable and hopeless woes. As I waved it there a warm hand grasped it, and I was addressed in English. So long had I avoided that language, it sounded like a foreign tongue to me. In my wildness I thought that I was dead, and that it was my father who addressed me. The voice told me to get up. I could not obey. Two men then carefully lifted and bore me to a carriage, and I was conveyed to a warm room, where cordials were administered to me, and I fell into a comfortable slumber, from which, after a few hours, I awoke considerably renewed. The presence of Englishmen was like introducing me to the home of my youth, and—strange aberration—it sent a flush of joy through my soul.

Directly I was informed of the circumstances which had led to my rescue.

A bachelor uncle of mine, on the maternal side, had lately died, leaving by will a small annuity to me. Inquiry had been made concerning my whereabouts; and after diligent search I had been traced to Germany. There they found me as I have described. Whence the scrupulous honesty which had actuated the apparently disinterested administrators, I never troubled myself much to discover. Perhaps, my mother from paradise accompanied them. I have often thought so. Yet, perhaps, it is only superstition. But I do love to think of my mother, my father, my wife, my child, as looking down kindly and lovingly from their beatitude, upon the wretched wanderer.

Under the kind administerings of my new friends, I soon recovered my usual strength, and with it, a decided change came over me, which was not altogether owing to my altered situation and returning health. I had a kind of half consciousness that I had in part atoned for my crime and was forgiven. It gave me cheerfulness for a time, and I readily consented to return to England.

Accordingly, in company with my two friends, I embarked for London. As I approached the well-remembered shores, my gloom returned. I strove to resist it in vain. It increased upon me as I walked along the familiar streets. The places hallowed in my recollection by the innocence of my childhood, and youth seemed to look with sadness upon me. I did not dare to renew my old social relations, and cared not to form new ones. The two friends who had accompanied me from Germany, separated from me soon, and went away to their homes. I supported my increasing loneliness for a while, loth to venture again upon distant wanderings; but at last became convinced that no other course would save me from intolerable wretchedness. Having come into full possession of the annuity, I took passage for this country, where I arrived a little upwards of two years since. I seek the turmoil of large cities to divert the current that ever rushes darkly up to overwhelm me. Yet, sometimes a tender melancholy, soothing like the singing voices of angels—Oh! I know it is from those who love me—takes possession of me, and then I seek such wilds as these.

This is my story, gentlemen. The pain it has given me to relate it, and which I have tried in vain to avoid manifesting, may be to you a pledge of its truth. Alas! I would it were but idle fiction.

CHAPTER III.

When the narrator had ceased speaking, he covered his withered face with his withered hands, breathing heavily. The rest of us were all deeply moved, some shedding tears, the jolly-looking bald-headed man quite profusely, being obliged to use his pocket-handkerchief. For several minutes, no one seemed disposed to interrupt the tide of sympathetic sadness which prevailed. At last the president remarked abruptly, smiting his thigh—"Gentlemen, I don't know how you view it, but I say this is rather too serious. It chokes me, I vow! I've heard hard stories in my day, stories that made rough-skinned juries cry; but I'm inclined to think this is a little the hardest yet. I propose the card be turned. Let's try again. Let's see," looking around, "who is to tell the next one? I mo— but stop, I forgot, I'm president. Let some one motion to the desired effect."

"I motion," said the Quaker, "that the president himself favor us with the next effort."

"That's taking hold of the bridle-rein, my dear sir," responded that functionary. "I see sir, you haven't forgot our dispute an hour or two since. You want to be revenged, eh?"

"I second the motion," put in one of the farmer-like looking men, excited.

"Moved and seconded, then. I see it is inevitable —but, by-the-by, I have doubts of the regularity of this proceeding; at all events you should allow a fellow chance to stump it a little, particularly when he *wants* to be defeated."

"Go on sir," playfully commanded the Quaker. "Do your duty."

The motion was put, and unanimously carried. Whereupon the president arose, and with a loud voice demanded if any one would volunteer to treat the company to cigars.

"Cheerfully" said I, also rising, "I am yet indebted to you all." The little dry man remained apparently unconscious of what was going on; but the rest silently acquiesced, and we were soon seated again, industriously smoking.

"You still insist, do you?" asked the president of the Quaker.

"Indeed I do. Have you ever had a doubt that the majority can rule in a Republican government?"

"Well, then, prepare. It may take me some time; and as its getting late, I want all to assume a position in which you may fall asleep without interrupting the thread of my narrative, if sleep *should* overtake you, you understand."

In order to humor the joke, and not knowing how much unlike a joke it might turn out to be, each one adjusted himself in the most comfortable position allowed by circumstances, and, with eyes expectant, beheld the upright president, who, seeing the coast was clear, commenced as follows:—

Our unfortunate friend here, has given us a general autobiography. To entertain us, he has drawn from his own experience. For me to follow him with an empty bar-room yarn, would be ungenerous to him, and would probably grate harshly upon your ears. I will not do it. I, too, will tell you of what I have both seen and heard. Yet less generous than our unhappy friend, I shall confine my narration to six or seven years of my life. These years, though usually that most uninteresting lapse between boyhood and manhood, have been to me by far the most eventful which I have lived. Sadly eventful, alas! By the by, I complained of the seriousness of the story we have just heard. If I enter upon this rehearsal, I don't know that I shall better the matter; perhaps you do not feel as I did in regard to that story. I will take it for granted, that you do not, without asking you, and go on, having started, though I do wish I had something more cheerful to relate. But to the tale, or we shall never reach the end.

I was a hard boy, as you may guess from my make, perverse and boisterous. My father was a farmer, and my mother a farmeress, both of them contented to plough, sow, reap, and bring forth. And being industrious, they ploughed much, sowed much, and being under the immediate smile of Providence, they reaped abundant harvests, and brought forth many. I was the oldest of the flock—and a flock it was, except myself, who only wore the outer vestments. I budded and expanded under the fiery wrath and indignation of my father, who, being reserved and taciturn, and also very methodic, found me ever a buffeting thorn. I increased lustily, however, under the gleaming orbs, and sharp pruning tongue, and at the age of fourteen, embraced the notion that I was a man. Concerning this, my father and I fell out more malignantly than ever. But I cherished my new-blown dignity, and would not yield. The up-shot of it was, I clandestinely left the parental roof. It was a bad move, and I found it out very soon. Having never been away from home over night, and scarcely over a meal before, I had not imbibed the idea of providing for the future; and discovered the very first day, that my capital was altogether inadequate to the investment. The first twenty-four hours consumed my money, and I was thrown upon my spontaneous resources, which did not prove very fruitful. However, with a piece of bread begged here, and a bowl of milk begged there, I managed to keep my stomach tolerably quiet, and my feet comparatively active, until I had put a hundred miles between me and my old home. I landed, and stranded, the tenth morning from launching—speaking after the manner of the sea—in the city of New York. Here my manhood suffered great depreciation. I became immediately so completely merged and submerged, that I lost my identity,—so much so, that a little *hocus-pocus* would have convinced me that I had no existence at all, except in my eyes. As night came on, I began to get hungry. As soon as I began to think of food, I lost interest in everything else, and directed every sense and energy to finding some; and no wonder. I had tasted of nothing but my own spittle, and some pine splinters, since the night before. While bent vigorously upon the one thing needful, to me just then, I became infested with an exceedingly painful doubt. How was I to obtain possession of food, when I should have found it? I had not one cent, and my clothes were too dirty to offer in exchange. But neither did the doubt, nor the speculations that followed it, at all appease my appetite; and in view of the imperative necessity, I finally concluded that if from what I *knew* the case was doubtful, there was a great deal I did not know, and perhaps amongst that might be found means of escape from the present difficulty. Comforted, I wandered on.

At length, fearing that I should not be able even to find food by my own unaided efforts, I accosted a ragged, dirty urchin in size about four years old. "Bub," said I patronizingly, "can you tell me where I can get something to eat?"

"Bub!" he responded, swelling like a little toad. "Do you go to h—l, or I'll *bub* ye," looking fiercely and steadily up into my face. I slowly inserted my hands in my pantaloons pockets, and wonderingly returned his gaze.

"It's something you want to eat, heh?" he continued. "Look straight across this here street, will ye?"

I looked.

"Do you see tnat are sign, there?"

I had seen it before he asked me. It read in flaming red letters, in semi-circle, high on a post, "City Eating House." Strange as it may seem, still it is a fact, that, so slim was my worldly experience, and particularly the city part thereof, I interpreted that sign to signify an establishment kept and provided by the city for the benefit of those who could not pay. Fully possessed with this idea, I crossed the street, and boldly entering, made known my voracious want.

"Of course, sir; with all dispatch, sir. Sit down,

sir—at this table, sir. Any preference in dishes, sir?"

Good Lord! such politeness! It astounded me. I thought I had landed in paradise, surely. I thanked the genteel individual with considerable feeling, and allowed him to conduct me to a small round table, in a curtained recess, for the moment forgetting why I was there.

"Any preference in dishes?" repeated the obsequious gentleman.

I had none. In a few minutes a most tempting display covered the table, which I proceeded to demolish—not the table, but the fixins—with inexpressible relish. I ate long and fiercely; and came out, at last, appeased, with my face very red and greasy. I walked up and down the long room, wondering at the benevolence of those who kept so splendid an establishment for the indigent.

After completing my survey, I very properly thought about finding a place to sleep. I could see no chance for it there, and I turned my steps towards the door. Just as I reached it I was touched gently on the shoulder, and had my attention directed to a counter, with a man behind it, in a distant corner of the room. The man behind the counter was beckoning to me; and with a sense of doing some one a service, I went towards him. I approached and leaned against the counter.

"Two shillings, sir," said he, without looking at me.

I thought he must be addressing some one else, and looked around to see who it was.

"Two shillings, sir," he said again, looking at me.

"Me?" I asked; "I haven't got any money."

"No money? You young devil, you; do you suppose you are to eat your supper at our expense? Why, what do you mean, you infernal scapegrace! Call the policeman, Jim."

Now I did not know positively what 'policeman' meant; but guessed. "I did not mean to do any harm, sir; indeed I did not," I commenced, beseechingly.

"No words, you young scamp. No getting up a booboo, here."

Jim left ostensibly for a policeman, and I was left in a dismal fix, that's certain. While in the midst of this dilemma—both horns of which, as it were, thrust under my fifth ribs—an old sailor slid up to the counter, and wiping his greasy lips on his jacket.

sleeve, demanded "the bearing of that are reckoning o' yourn." While the score was being reckoned, he looked up, then around a great way off, as though searching for some distant object, then down, and his eyes settled on me.

"What's in the wind, lad," said he, compassionately; "aground?"

I chokingly told him I was out of money, and they were going to put me in jail.

"From the country, I reckon. Great way from port, perhaps?"

I answered meekly, "Yes."

He looked up, and then away to a great distance, again. "Say, you there, behind there, reckon in this lad's damage," at the same time throwing a gold coin upon the counter. The change was counted out, and the old sailor, grabbing up one handful and putting it in his own pocket, drew off the remainder into the other hand, and opening one of my trowsers pockets, shook it in there.

"Now, lad, bear up alongside, and we'll go aboard."

The phraseology was so entirely new, and so radically differed from what I was accustomed to hearing, that it conveyed no definite idea to my understanding, which fact must have been manifested by my coun tenance, for I said nothing.

"Poor fellow!" he continued. "You don't understand. I mean, will ye go with me?" His manner had inspired me with confidence in him, and thinking he might assist me in getting a place to sleep, I followed him. It was quite dark, and as we went along he took hold of my hand. Assured by his kindness, I ventured to ask him where he was going.

"On board for the night. Ye must go with me, and I'll give ye a hammock."

I informed him I had been to supper.

"Hammock, hammock, lad; a place to sleep. Bless you! I knowed ye had been to supper. That was what he dog behind there was snarling about, wasn't it."

Depressed with shame at my ignorance, I made no further remarks, and we soon came to the wharf.

"Keep a steady lookout as ye climb this here," cautioned my guide, as we walked up a narrow plank, leading to the midships of a huge merchant vessel, darkly looming against the sky. I took his caution to heart, and carefully ascending, found myself for the first time in a ship. My first general impression was of being in a grocery of indefinite extent—such piles of boxes, and barrels, and sacks; such a profusion of what seemed to me tar, molasses, and flour on the floor; such a redolence of indistinguishable smells;—I was quite bewildered and impressed with awe. I followed the sailor passively, who conducted me along a winding way, walled narrowly in with innumerable boxes and sacks, to a low apartment which he introduced to me as the "steerage." Here I had ocular demonstration of what a hammock was; and blushing at the recollection of my ignorance, I submitted to the kind direction of my protector, and was soon asleep.

I was aroused at break of day by the old sailor—whom I shall call Senk, for that was the name he went by—who, when he perceived I was fully awake, proceeded to admonish me as to what my future conduct must be—first, however, ascertaining my precise relations to existing circumstances and to the world at large.

"Ye must say 'sir' to everybody that speaks to ye. Be most devilish civil, and out o' the way. The officers are a most damned impudent set. They'd kick ye overboard in a minute if they'd happen to stumble or slip, and you'd laugh the least bit or snicker. And be sure ye always be very particular to say 'Captain Smith' to the man ye hear me call so. Now mind that; it's very important. I want you to stay on board, and be a sailor. You can't do better. I brought a fellow on here five years ago, and there ain't a better sailor ever climbed the rigging. Wouldn't ye like to be a sailor, lad, eh?" he concluded, getting up a little sham enthusiasm for the occasion.

I had not left home with the intention of going to sea. But the experience of the previous night had disgusted me with the city, and between my disgust and a certain vague inclination to visit distant lands I came suddenly and decidedly to the conclusion that I would be a sailor. Senk, who had scrutinized my countenance in the most lively manner during the short cogitation that had passed within me, saw instantly my decision, and without waiting for me to speak, burst forth rapturously—

"Ay, ay, sir. I knowed you'd do it. Now come along wi' me on the hurrican deck, and mind ye do jest as I tole ye."

I submitted to his leading, and we went up on deck.

As we were walking slowly along, a little bare grey head with spectacles, popped up from a square hole about three steps off from us.

"On board eh?" it said, adding a pair of broad shoulders to it.

"Ay, ay, sir, Captain Smith," promptly responded Senk. "Been on over night."

"Well, that's strange. Got kicked out for disorderly conduct somewhere, I suppose, and couldn't stay ashore. Thank God! we're to leave to morrow."

While giving utterance to these amiable remarks, the head and shoulders, which Senk had called "Captain Smith," built themselves up heavily, and revealed a quite unsymmetrical foundation, based with a pair of remarkably large feet. Fairly established on deck, he directly made a discovery.

"What have you got here, you old hull?"

"A young lad in trouble, that I picked up ashore last night," commenced Senk.

"I'll warrant. You are always up to such foolery. Mighty benevolent at others' expense! What do you expect to do here, young man?" he continued, addressing me, and evidently meaning no respect by the title.

"I don't know, sir—C-Captain Smith, ah!" I emitted, borne down with awe.

Though naturally bold, and inconsiderate, either of times or circumstances, when at home among the well-known cows, horses, and school-boys, I had seen so much in the short interval since leaving the parental roof which demonstrated my own weakness, that I had not only lost every vestige of my supposed manhood, but had, as it were, been born again, and was scarcely advanced beyond infancy. My confusion was very great, which I suppose somewhat flattered the august Captain Smith, who went on to say, in a milder tone, after a few moments' reflection, "Do you want to go to sea?"

Raising my eyes to the feet of the awful man, I replied "Yes," forgetting to add the title until he commenced speaking again, which caused an additional dash of confusion, so completely bewildering me that I lost all he said, until he shifted his remarks to Senk.

"Take him below, Senk, and tell the steward I sent him."

Glad to get from the oppressive presence, I followed Senk with alacrity.

I found the steward, to whom Senk ceremoniously

presented me, a large, heavy-looking gentleman of color. He had a mild, placid expression all over him, that made me feel quite at home. We directly fell into conversation, and became rapidly acquainted. He patiently pointed out my duties, and on my performing one of them successfully, he promptly dubbed me "Cabin Boy," nicknaming me Phil, and I swore allegiance to him, and through him to the ship; and from that hour forth reckoned myself a sailor.

The next day, in fulfillment of the gratefully expressed prediction of Captain Smith, we set sail. The vessel was bound for Quilimane, on the eastern coast of Africa, and was heavily laden. The first three weeks after leaving the last American port were very monotonous. An annoying alternation of spasmodic winds and dead calms rendered our progress slow and uncertain. We had been out of sight of land about ten days, the great sea alone all around us, the sun rising and setting in it, the scattered clouds coming out of and disappearing in it,—when one morning at break of day those of us who were sleeping were startled from our slumbers by the heavy roll of distant thunder. I jumped from my hammock, and went on deck. The whole aspect of things was changed. The solemn ocean had assumed a new, and it seemed to me ominous hue, and appeared smaller, like, I could not help thinking, a monstrous serpent contracted for a spring. In the western sky were new clouds, some of them thick and almost black, others tinged with the prismatic hues of a summer sunrise, and the clear blue sky was nowhere to be seen The atmosphere, too, was changed. It was heavy; and the scream of a sea-bird—whence no one could tell—came painfully distinct to the ear.

About sun an hour high, Captain Smith came on deck. A smart, east wind had sprung up since sunrise, and we were making a long tack to the southward of our course, which was southeast, under full sail. He went aft, and with his long glass scanned the western sky very carefully several minutes. He then went to the wheel, and examined the ropes. Apparently satisfied with his examination, he next went forward, and shouted to the lookout aloft—
"Keep a sharp eye ahead, there, do you hear?"

"Ay, ay, sir."

Then taking a general survey from where he stood, of the vessel, he turned to Mr. Demt, the first mate, who, by the way, was a very obsequious, no-minded sort of individual, and said in a low, serious tone, "We shall be a good hundred knots from this point before sundown, or some fathoms below low-water mark, I can tell you that."

"That's my opinion, Captain Smith," said Mr. Demt, looking towards the west.

I beheld these significant manœuvres, and listened to this remark of Captain Smith with the profoundest interest. Something awful was portending, I had no doubt, but of what it was, precisely, I had only a vague idea. To be sure, things looked ominously strange; yet I had seen similar appearances on shore pass into a clear day, or into a dull three-days' rain. Captain Smith's conduct, however, could not be without a cause, thought I; and the recollection of what I had heard about storms at sea, coming up in this connection, shed some light and a good deal of dread into my mind. While I was yet undetermined how to set the matter down in my judgment, it thundered again, a long, low, heavy roll, as though it were under water, deep down, and rising with heavy sweeps to the surface. The clouds in the west grew rapidly thicker and more cumbrous, rising slowly, and sending out torn fragments, which, reaching in long stretches far towards the east, began to darken the sun. Another deep roll of thunder, heavier, harsher than before, and the wind suddenly ceased. The long pennant fell, and the huge sails flapped listlessly against the masts. Captain Smith, who had been a short time below, now came hurriedly on deck with a speaking trumpet in his hand.

"All hands into the rigging!" he shouted fiercely. "Up! up! every one of you, and work like devils. Furl every rag." Then, turning to the first mate, he said—"I fear this ought to have been done before. At all events we have not one minute to lose."

"That's my opinion, Captain Smith," echoed the other.

At this crisis I was beckoned below by the benign steward. In the unusual circumstances that were transpiring, I had forgotten my official duties, which I now hastened to dispatch, and came again on deck just in time to see the men hurrying from the bare masts and yards, like so many frightened pigeons from a dry tree, some flushed with agreeable expectation, others pale with fear.

The sky was now completely overcast, and every few moments lurid flashes filled the whole scene, while the deep, heavy thunder rolled almost continually. Absorbed in watching the movements on deck, I did not notice that Senk stood by me, until he said, grasping my shoulder with one hand rather harshly, and pointing with the other towards the west, "See there, lad." I looked. There was a long streak of white extending to the right and left out of sight. It was rapidly approaching, and seemed to annihilate the sea as it came. "What is that?" I exclaimed. A deep roar, faint, yet heavy, from the direction of the appearance answered me. It was the vanguard of the coming storm. I looked in Senk's face. It was pallid. "Are we going to be wrecked?" said I, trembling with apprehension.

"I don't know, lad," he replied swallowing. "That's the worst looking storm *I* ever seen, I know; if we don't founder, there's a chance."

We both looked in silence a few moments at the awfully portentous object that was so rapidly and irresistibly nearing. Suddenly Senk started, and taking me by the hand said—"Farewell! my lad. There'll be no chance for words when that's upon us. If we go down, farewell!—ye'd better go below."

I don't know why it was, but I had an exceeding

repugnance to going below, and therefore told Senk I would rather stay on deck.

"Hang on, then," he said; "ye think ye've been pulled; but ye'll find ye never was pulled so before." With this he left me, but returned almost immediately with a lanyard.

"If ye *will* stay up here, ye must be tied," he said, leading me to a mast, and proceeding to make me fast to it.

Nearer, ever more swiftly approaching, came that ominous shape; and now I could see the sea beyond. All was one white sheet of foam. Nearer, nearer it came. Nearer. Now close at hand. I was rigid with suspense. A moment. The long pennant starts like an unsheathed sword, keen, quick, glancing off, and pointing with quivering end; the tall masts bend; the huge ship of a thousand tons, now like a feather, rises upon the sweeping billows, and the storm is upon us.

Gentlemen, I can assure those of you who have not experienced it, that you can form no just idea of what a strong wind at sea is. It does not seem like wind, but like thin water, rushing in an overwhelming, resistless tide. So fierce and swift is it, that the skin exposed fairly smarts. Quite painfully did mine smart, as strapped to that mast I stood, or, rather hung, helpless. For a full minute, I believe, I could get no breath at all. At length, by putting my hands over my mouth, and turning my face to leeward, I managed to breathe after a gasping fashion.

With the same tremendous force the wind continued for nearly an hour. The vessel obeying her rudder faithfully, shot along at an alarming speed. The wind slacked a little, and but a little, and the sea began to rise fearfully. The two men at the wheel were found inadequate, and two more were called to their assistance. The waves increased every moment, dashing wildly along, without beginning or end, exhaustless. The noble ship reeled and plunged like a wounded war-horse, yet still held on her course.

It was not long before I fully realized the importance of being secured as I was. A great wave, threefold larger than any before, came sweeping along. "A sea! a sea!" shouted the men at the wheel in chorus, "A sea! a sea!" was echoed from all parts of the deck. I drew in a full breath, and embraced the mast. The next instant a tide ten feet above our heads dashed madly over us. The good ship swayed as though, endowed with life, she had been dealt a stunning blow. Would she go down? The thought was scarcely formed when I was again breathing the misty air. Every movable had been swept away; and scarcely had the water subsided, when the heart-thrilling cry rose above the storm. "A man overboard!" Why raise that cry? Poor wretch! how could they save him? He was a young sailor, inexperienced in such dreadful straits. They tried to save him. He was seen floating a short distance away. Being a good swimmer, he sustained himself bravely; but the cruel tide had borne him too far from the ship. A rope was thrown, but he could not reach it. "A sea! a sea!" cried the men at the wheel, and another wave, like the first, dashed over us. The man overboard was gone for ever.

I began to wish myself below. Matters had put on a more serious aspect than I had anticipated. But a few moments' reflection convinced me that the attempt would be absurd; so I grinned defiance to my fears, and stood prepared for whatever dispensation it should please Providence to inflict.

The wind now shifted suddenly, blowing at a sharp

angle with the previous track, and the waves became smaller, but more terrible. The ship tossed frantically. No more obeying the rudder, she floated unmanageable, creaking, and straining as though every moment she would part asunder. Again the wind shifted, and became fitful. One fierce gust carried away the main-top-mast, with a tearing crash heard clearly above the rushing, deafening sound of the wind and waves. The tightly furled sails began to loosen, by slow degrees at first, though the wind snatched as with a thousand giant fingers—then gave way, gasket by gasket, till, flapping and tearing, they were carried away, leaving bare poles. It was now nearly noon. Every change so far had been for the worse, and our prospects were growing more dubious every moment. As the last sail—which clung long, like hope—was flying in shreds, I saw Captain Smith shake hands with Mr. Demt, who had been continually at his side, and go below. He had not been gone three minutes when Senk came rushing by me, and leaped down the hatchway. I looked to the fore top. The lookout, stationed there, was waving his hat, and shouting, his face purple with exertion. What can it mean? I inquired anxiously of myself,

While I was looking, and striving to form some conjecture, the sound of Captain Smith's big feet on the deck near me, attracted my attention. He was running towards the bow. I had never before seen him run, and for the moment, anxious as I was, I felt strongly inclined to laugh, so ludicrous was the general impression his figure made upon me. Arrived at the bow, he clapped his glass to his eye. Not being satisfied with his position, he came back, and boldly mounted the shrouds, which led to the lookout. I expected every instant to see him fall, the ship plunged so dreadfully. But he reached the cross-trees in safety, and putting the glass again to his eye, he looked, while the lookout, now more at ease, sat with both hands partly raised, as though he were holding the ship, sea, winds, and all things, that Captain Smith might look. He evidently saw something. His hat blew off. Still he continued to look. A sudden lurch of the vessel made him, perhaps for the first time in his life, drop his glass. The wind bore it like a thread far out into the water. Still he continued to look.

"Our time's come," shouted some one in my leeward ear. It was Senk.

"What is it? what is it?" I shouted in reply.

"A reef lies directly across her course. No chance now."

The consciousness of Senk's long experience on the sea, left in me no room for doubt, and the horrors of immediate death came upon me. For a moment I was paralyzed. Yet, but a moment; for my mind, reacting from the shock, became as a mirror, upon which all my past life shone a living picture. I saw my father and mother; my younger brothers and sisters, and myself—rash, thoughtless boy—among them, and my schoolmates playing at their exciting games. The fields where I had labored in discontent were before me; and the patient oxen that had so often been visited with my wrath; the cows, the sheep, the lazy swine, and the rampant calves; the old church, and the stereotyped divine who had warned the young goats—of which I was chief—so often to beware; the quiet churchyard—and with that I recurred to things around me. I thought of how my father and my mother now looked, and my brothers and sisters; how they would never know what became of me, ever hoping that I would return, yet hoping in vain. Thus wandering in a reverie, insensible to the drenching spray and to the extreme fatigue which my unchanging position occasioned me, my eyes were attracted by an appearance directly ahead and not far off, which resembled the one that had characterized the approaching storm. I turned. Senk still stood by me. "What's that?" I asked, forgetting what he had told me a few minutes before, and vaguely anticipating a counter storm. He made no reply. He, too, was perhaps thinking of a quiet home far away, where knelt aged parents at the close of day, to ask protection for one who had gone forth upon the treacherous deep. I repeated my question in a higher tone.

"That white streak?" he inquired, looking intently in the direction I pointed. "Yes, that's the reef, Good God! we're close upon it. Say your prayers, lad. It will soon be too late."

Captain Smith had continued to look all this time. Perhaps *he* had thoughts of home. But whatsoever occupied his mind, was to appearance suddenly dispelled when the sun, now past the meridian, flashed out from the clouds which were much broken, and shone down upon the appalling danger ahead. He left his position, and descending to the deck, went aft. If I had dared, I would have unfastened myself, and followed him, for I felt attracted towards him in this awful extremity. But it required all the skill of an experienced sailor to walk that deck at that time, and I did not deem it prudent for me to venture.

One by one the remainder of the crew came up from below, the placid steward bringing up the rear. He came alongside of me, and said in a voice as calm as the exertion necessary to make me hear allowed—"Well, they say we've got to go down to the bottom; are you prepared to die?"

In foolish moments I had made sport of his pious turn of mind, laughing at his laudations of the enthusiastic sect to which he belonged—he was a devout Methodist—and whistling discord to his psalmodic efforts, in which he indulged night and morning; but now, in my despair, I strove to lean upon his honest piety.

"Good man, pray for me," I cried piteously. Obedient to my wish he knelt, and offered a short petition to Heaven, of which I heard not a word because of the confusion that prevailed. As he arose, I could not help perceiving the contrast he presented to the rest of the crew. Despair was stamped upon each countenance. Some were crying toward Heaven with beseeching looks, and uplifted hands, others were walking to and fro gnashing their teeth, others again sat with hands convulsively clenched in their hair, and staring vacantly. He, the steward, alone was calm; the derided "St. Ebony," as he had been often termed, leaning upon the Power which is not of this world, stood sublimely there, a man among those shrinking wretches.

While observing thus the contrast, I saw Mr. Demt make a motion as though suggesting something to Captain Smith, who was leaning against the quarter-rail. He immediately took the glass which Mr. Demt handed him, and looked long and intently in a direction contrary to the danger; then, in answer to the anxiously inquiring gaze of his companion, he shook his head.

The wind veered again, apparently so as to blow us the more disastrously upon the reef—the sound of whose breakers was plainly heard—and continuing steadily for about five minutes, ceased almost as abruptly as it had begun. Not so the sea. Lashed for six hours so unsparingly by the fleet giant, it would not be lulled by the soft breeze that followed.

"What's to be done?" said Captain Smith to Mr. Demt, as they walked slowly past me, forward.

"That's just what I was thinking, Captain Smith," replied the addressed.

"I don't see as anything can be done," rejoined Captain Smith. "There's not time to do anything, if there were any use in trying. We must go aground—I can see no help for it."

"That's just my opinion, Capt. Smith," said Mr. Demt; and they walked out of my hearing.

Lurching, plunging, drifting slowly, we approached the reef. Again Capt. Smith leaned over the quarter rail and looked. The sun was shining most brilliantly, the sky being perfectly clear. Shifting his glass from eye to eye, and wiping it often, then removing it, and, squaring himself, re-adjusting it several times, as though taking aim, Captain Smith at last threw up his hands with a dignified gesture. Mr. Demt walked hurriedly to him, and taking the glass, looked. The boatswain and two or three sailors now joined them, and the attention of all was attracted towards their movements. Senk stood not far from me. "Is there any hope?" I inquired. Before he could reply, a new, joyful cry burst from all sides—"A sail! a sail!" I looked towards the group. Captain Smith was smiling most cordially, and shaking hands with the obsequious mate, down whose cheeks ran tears. "Thank God! thank God!" sounded from all sides. The pious steward was more ceremonious in his gratitude. He knelt upon the deck and poured out his soul quite devoutly, though the motion of the vessel thwarted his devotions most sadly.

After the first gush, the joyous excitement on board ebbed greatly. Of what practical use was that sail to us? was the substance of every one's thoughts. It was yet far distant—barely discernible with the naked eye—and in a few minutes, at most, we would be scattered among the greedy, remorseless waves. To add to the returning depression, it was determined that, by the course the stranger was taking, she would be out of sight in an hour.

Could we attract their notice?

The gun was thought of, but instantly pronounced inexpedient. Other things were thought of, and mentioned, and some one was speaking, when, borne on a heavy sea, the ship struck with tremendous force.

Grating, and tearing, she floated off with the ebbing billow; and before we had fairly recovered our breath, she struck again,—this time with a crash that sent all traces of blood from the faces of the bravest; even the steward, for the moment, appeared slightly faded. Again, the third time. She did not float away. Another sea followed, and hove her huge bulk further on to the unyielding reef. Another, and another. She poised a few moments, as though, entirely exhausted with the merciless conflict, the last struggle had come, then sank heavily and helplessly upon her side, a forlorn wreck. Fortunately for me, the side of the mast I occupied proved the upper side. Had it been the under, I must have perished. As it was, every wave dashed over me, and I should not have lived five minutes, had it not been for Senk and the steward, who, foreseeing the danger, had secured a lanyard. With their united efforts,—the steward holding and Senk descending—I was, nearly strangled, brought to the bulwarks, and bidden to hold on for my life.

The sea had become considerably calmed, but it still ran high enough to dash over the wreck from time to time, sunken as it was in about two fathoms of water. However, the evil was lessening, and hope stimulated us to efforts that seemed like the efforts of despair. While we were thus clinging to the shattered and swaying wreck, the sun went down into the ragged bosom of the sea; and as the twilight, softened by the coming night, enabled us to see the horizon clearly, we saw—how very grateful was the sight!—we saw that the stranger had altered her course, and was approaching us. While the first thrill of joy was yet trembling along our nerves, Captain Smith, removing the glass through which he had been looking for a few minutes, said, with a familiar cheerfulness so unusual with him that some of us at first failed to apprehend,—"Boys, she has a signal out! She sees us!" Rapturous joy now took possession of us all. The good steward thanked his Maker seven or eight times, in slow, emphatic succession, and pulled out a pocket volume of hymns essaying a song of praise; but the sea, unmindful of him, sent a great wave that swallowed up his book, and he gave up the attempt.

As the darkness deepened, and the twilight faded, we saw, dimmer and dimmer, the friendly sail approaching; and as the new moon dipped slowly into the sea, which was very much calmed from sunset, we saw that sail quite distinctly still approaching.

A long night was that. Exhausted by labor and want of food, it was a wonder that we sustained ourselves in our critical position through the long, dark hours. But we did, without the loss of a man; and when the morning twilight opened the prospect, we saw the stranger vessel at anchor a half mile from us, and a small boat, manned with four vigorous oarsmen, coming to our relief.

Before nine o'clock we were all on board; and having refreshed ourselves with a most relishable breakfast, we gathered on deck, contemplating our last night's lodgings quite seriously, for we had many regrets. Senk actually shed tears, declaring that he would rather have buried his mother than seen his home for so many years lying there helpless, to be knocked in pieces by the next storm that should come that way. I shed some tears with him; and he was yet narrating to me, in a feeling manner, how the staunch old vessel had bravely stood the onset and the angry buffetings of the last storm of her course, when the brisk order was given to make ready for departure. Senk left the sentence unfinished in his mouth, and the next instant was at the capstan, heaving with might and main, and joining lustily in the exhilarating chorus.

Soon all was ready, and slowly we left the scene of so much hope and despair, gathering aft, as the distance increased, to catch a parting glimpse of the wreck, and straining our eyes till the sharpest sighted declared it no longer visible.

CHAPTER IV.

At the point where the foregoing chapter ends, the narrator was interrupted in his story, by the little dry man rising, and stating, apologetically, that, as his plan of travel rendered it necessary for him to depart at a very early hour, he must, though somewhat against his inclination, for he was considerably interested in the narration, and hoped it would continue to prove entertaining to us,—he must, however, with our permission, retire to bed.

We all assented by rising; and, the Quaker setting the example, we approached severally, and taking his withered hand, bade the unhappy man farewell. When we had resumed our positions, and all was still again, the supposed lawyer, after clearing his throat, sonorously continued his story as follows:—

The stranger that had come so opportunely to our assistance, was also a trading vessel, and belonged to a company in Liverpool. It was bound for the same port for which our ill-fated ship had been destined—a fortunate incident for Captain Smith, and Mr. Demt, who had friends there, but of no account to the rest of us, as our home was the deep, and our friends its wandering denizens, met—it mattered not where. Of course, I do not apply this last remark to myself, so much as the rest of the crew, though I have since had occasion to feel its truth somewhat.

I had hitherto served as cabin-boy, and owing to the amiable disposition of my master, had not experienced much hardship. So pleasant indeed had been my situation, that I had congratulated myself often in view of it—especially as compared with the tasks and oppression of my earlier boyhood. But in the change of circumstances, generally, mine changed also. On board the new ship, I was placed "before the mast," and promptly initiated into the calling of a common sailor. The sleight-of-foot which I had so often admired—dizzy with the contemplation, I was now forced to practice myself. Oh, it was trying! the first trembling essay to mount to the mast-head. I hardly think I should have accomplished it but for Senk, who volunteered to go up just before me. With the stimulus of his cheering voice, and the consciousness of his being at hand to assist in case of failure, I accomplished the feat in perfect safety, returning to the deck alone. Repeating the manœuvre often, I soon got the better of my fears, and felt entirely at ease anywhere, from the deck upwards, indefinitely. But the usual pleasing excitement arising from the overcoming of obstacles wore away directly, and I became exquisitely sensitive to the galling chain of monotonous labor imposed upon me. The weather was generally disagreeable, being windy, and wet, in that half-way manner, which forbids alike ease or excitement, and being fixedly on duty twelve hours out of the twenty-four, without regard to external circumstances, my cup of affliction filled up rapidly, and I felt all the nameless agonies of an oppressed boy. I sickened at heart, and soured in the same locality; and in the course of fermentation I thought much and lovingly of my old home. I thought of it more and more until my absence of mind attracted the notice of my companions; and the happy turns of speech which some of them contributed at my expense, considerably heightened the prevailing state of mind under which I labored. Yet Senk stood by me, and com forted me hopefully. Had it not been for him, I might have gone down under the load. But his kindness did not hinder my being seized finally with home-sickness, in one of its most demolishing forms.

Home-sickness! thou pale-faced embodiment of fond regrets, hovering over the weary and oppressed, far from the roof that echoed the cries of their infancy,—hovering kindly with an aroma emanating from thee which embalms the scenes which fond memory brings,—touching with soft, feeble fingers the heartstrings. O, thou — but I will not tarry hoping to grow eloquent. Suffice it to say, that I was growing worse daily, when a decided circumstance put an end to my ailment, quite magically—at once, and for ever. It was this:

One sunny afternoon, soon after doubling Cape Good Hope—by-the-by, the first sunshine we had been visited with for three weeks—I was sitting on the taffrail thinking of the sunny afternoons of my earlier life. The genial rays of the sun gave the run of my mind a dreamy character, separating me quite distinctly from surrounding things. From reverie, encouraged by the silence and general harmony which prevailed, the transition to real sleep was quite easy and natural—so easy and natural, that I underwent it, and my centre of gravity being nicely adjusted, I remained wrapped in serene slumber for a time. As sleep deepened upon me, my muscles insensibly relaxed, particularly those of my arms and hands, which embraced my knees. Suddenly my fingers parted asunder, and with an unreserved lurch I departed headlong backwards into the sea. I came to the surface in a state of disputed possession between air and water—an idea of sharks, however, taking partial lead of my confused faculties, and imparting a spasmodic stimulus, I succeeded in maintaining my head, until a line, with a buoy attached, thrown to me from the receding ship, enabled my comrades to draw me in, which they did in silence until I was safely on deck; then transpired a great shout and a miscellaneous waving of tarpaulins which made me feel quite distinguished. The cure was perfect. I felt as though I had poured myself out a libation to the sea, and was thenceforth devoted to it.

Our voyage thenceforward was without accident or incident worthy of recapitulation. Arrived at the destined port, we, who had belonged to the wrecked vessel, went out two and two and separated, some of us for ever. Senk seemed to have incorporated me into the narrow sphere of his hopes and desires. He clung to me as a father to a child. Being without employment we set about seeking the same. We succeeded after some search in finding a vessel, which having in a late storm lost a part of her crew, accepted our proffered services with a promise of fair remuneration, and accordingly we went on board and took up quarters. It was an English vessel, not so large as the one we had quitted, but better appointed. It was engaged in the East India trade, and was on its way out, being only incidentally in that port for the purpose of refitting. At that time great danger from pirates was incurred in navigating some parts of the Indian Ocean, and every trading vessel was more or less provided with means of self-defence. Our ship carried four pieces of ordnance, and had also a small armory. These I discovered the next day after going on board, while perambulating, cat-fashion, for the purpose of forming more intimate acquaintance with my new home; and I also discovered some marks which suggested an idea of war. I asked a sailor who stood near as to their origin. From him I learned that the ship had already seen two desperate conflicts with pirates, and had been metaphorically named 'The Irresistible,' on account of having come off conqueror both times. I swung in my hammock that night to the imaginary cadence of imaginary fifes and drums, and saw in my dreams great fields of men mowed down, and the whole swallowed up in a shoreless sea of blood.

Our captain's name was Thims. He was as much the reverse of Captain Smith as was the orthography of his name. He was a tall, well-proportioned, robust, sunny man—everybody's friend as long as everybody would allow him to be, but a most implacable enemy to any one who saw fit to refuse him friendship. He was jovial among his shipmates to an uncommon degree, and strongly prepossessed in favor of the world at large. Every sailor on board, except one sulky old hound—of whom I shall have something to say by-and-by—was his familiar and ever cordially greeted friend; and so much was he beloved by them, that the fulfillment of his wishes was at all times a most binding duty among them.

Being duly refitted and rendered sea-worthy, our ship's prow was turned seaward, and we were soon again far out upon the deep.

Months passed. I continued to perform my nautical duties faithfully, and in a measure successfully, making great initiatory progress. Being quick and vigorous, I soon acquired all those tricks of ascent and descent, of balancing and turning summersault which so puzzle a landsman in a sailor, and could climb and leap, and swing, and shout "Ay, ay, sir!" with the lustiest. Everything went on smoothly. The vessel was duly freighted to the entire satisfaction of the agents employed by the house that owned her, and we turned prow towards London.

Our voyage to that commercial emporium was slow and quiet, without prominent incidents. It consumed several months.

Tarrying at London three or four weeks, we again put to sea. Again our voyage was prosperous, and tedious, until we reached the vicinity of Cape Good Hope. Here we met with a narrow escape. A sudden, rampant squall, peculiar to that coast, came up in the night, and blowing directly ashore, bore us unmercifully along with it. Happily, we were so far advanced upon our course as to have passed the worst part of the promontory; yet there was one rock, as it afterwards appeared, from which we were saved barely by one somewhat surprising circumstance. The sulky sailor, to whom I have before alluded, was at the wheel. He was a gigantic fellow, having fully the strength two ordinary men, and proud of his strength, or, rather, taking a malicious pleasure in exhibiting it, he would never brook the assistance of another in the discharge of his duties as helmsman. It was very dark. Captain Thims was on the quarter deck, attending to the report of soundings from the man in the main chains, when he perceived dimly a dark object to the starboard, which he took for a rock.

"Hard a-starboard! hard a-starboard!" he cried at the top of his voice.

"Ay, ay, sir," was the hoarse response, and the prow turned short, and plowed directly into, instead of away from, the dark object, while at the same instant, from larboard mid-ships, came the despairing cry—"A rock! a rock! we're lost!" But we were not lost. The dark object proved an illusion; the danger was opposite. The grim helmsman had saved us, though he had intended, as all thought, to dash the ship upon the rock. Why Captain Thims retained this man in his service I never knew. There seemed a bond between them, like the fabled bond which secured prospectively to His Satanic Majesty the souls of men. A more sincere, deep-rooted, infernal hatred could scarcely exist between two mortals, than exhibited itself now and then between them. Yet there were times when they walked arm in arm with each other, but as we might suppose embodied thunderbolts to walk arm in arm. On such occasions there was a pallor in the captain's face, and a most malignant frown on the face of the other, which it was frightful to behold. They were sometimes in the cabin by themselves for hours; and at such times, those who were near heard horrible, hissing words, and grating and gnashing of teeth. The grim giant would accept of no other situation than that of common sailor, though by experience, he was fully adequate to the command of any vessel in any latitude, the second mate said one day in my hearing, and I have no doubt that it was so. Altogether it was quite a mysterious affair, and gave rise to much rough speculation among the superstitious of our crew.

Except the narrow escape at the Cape there was

nothing occurred to mar or relieve the quiet monotony of our voyage, and we cast anchor one beautiful morning at sunrise, in the port of Borneo—which was the first point of destination.

We remained there nearly two months, much of the time idle, waiting for something, but no one could tell what, for all the freight we were to take on there was shipped during the first ten days of our stay. It was surmised, and quite loudly talked of, that "the Devil"—such was the expressive cognomen by which the giant sailor was known among us—had a hand in the unusual delay. How far this surmise was correct, may be inferred from the sequel.

Finally, after the long, long, and most tiresome waiting for what turned out to be literally nothing, so far as I could see or learn, the welcome order to weigh anchor was given. We hastened to obey it, and were soon ploughing away under full sail before a good breeze. We were bound thence for Manilla, there to complete our freight. A Spanish family had taken passage on board our vessel—a new circumstance, somewhat agreeably disturbing the usual routine of my previous life. It was a family of six—the father and mother middled-aged, of dignified demeanor, evidently accustomed from childhood to the careful observance of all the little decencies of life; a daughter and her husband, enjoying the first raptures of the honeymoon,—and well did those raptures become them;—a younger daughter in the bud of maidenhood, and a little ruddy-cheeked boy, seven or eight years old. They all spoke English with passable fluency, and during the day-time were much on deck, conversing with the captain and mates, and enjoying the grateful sea breezes. The bride attracted my attention particularly. I think in all my travels on this great globe, I have never met a being that has superseded, in my judgment, that gentle, beaming creature. Though so young at the time that I could only receive the impression without second thought, I have since speculated upon it seriously, and make my statement soberly. It was not so much owing to the regularity of her features, nor the melting contour of her harmonious form, that made her appear so very beautiful; it was the indescribable "general effect," as artists say,—the radiance of virgin passion just putting forth its last, ripest, richest beauties under the genial influence of kindred passion bestowed without reserve. The groom was a fit companion to her:—tall, with a noble and graceful bearing, he, too, was more graceful, more nobly beautiful for the passion that absorbed him. The younger daughter was a sweet, lovable girl, full of honest curiosity, which she so artlessly sought to gratify that she stood in constant need of check from her parents. She went about talking with everybody, asking a great many unnecessary, and sometimes unanswerable questions, yet expressing surprise so ingenuously, followed with such a sweet, playful smile, that it seemed a delightful privilege to answer her. She seemed at first to confine her investigations to the medium of the older sailors; but they soon took such a promiscuous character that *I* began to fear an approach. You must bear in mind that I was quite young then; and I was moreover very bashful in the presence of the other sex. In this case particularly so, as she walked about in my eyes almost an angel. My fears harrowed me so much that I became quite nervous, which illy prepared me for what actually happened. I was standing near Senk, to whom she was addressing some questions, importing a desire to know more explicitly the process of navigation by night. Having received the answers she desired, with the usual remunerating smile, she turned her beaming face full on me, and said, as though she hardly anticipated an answer, "Do you like to be a sailor?" If she did not expect reply, she was not disappointed, for in my confusion I could not utter a word. Seeming to take compassion upon my disturbed condition, she passed on, but presently returned, asking me, with a serious look, if I had any father and mother. During the minute that had elapsed, the first upheaval had subsided, and I quite calmly told her I had, and a sister, too, like her, far off in America. To this she replied, asking where America was,—then suddenly recollecting, she proceeded to answer herself, and went on to ask many questions about my home, which I answered very elaborately, and with much emotion. Then she told me about her home in Borneo; and she was yet telling me in a very animated manner about the garden she had there, when her mother called her, and they went below.

Gentlemen, I love the sunshine, and I approach darkness unwillingly. I love to recall that beam which for a brief space cheered my wandering boyhood; but the recollection of the darknes, that followed, has a deep shadow of terror to me, though a quarter of a century has passed since its awful folds blotted from the world, so much beauty and rapturous hope, so much rough, yet sterling integrity, and real, honest humanity. I would spare your hearts the recital, but you have required a story of me, and this is a part of it, and must be told.

It was a breezy evening in October, cool for that latitude. The day had closed with a doubtful sky. Big, detached clouds that seemed to have no water in them, yet were very thick and black, came, and passed on to the South steadily, and somewhat rapidly. We had been out from Borneo six days. The winds having been adverse, we had made slow progress, and were on that evening making a tack which was carrying us off the Eastern shore of Palawau. There was no land in sight. The sea was slightly ruffled, but only so much as to give a pleasant motion to the vessel, and the barometer indicating no change of weather for the present, a general quiet pervaded the whole ship's company. The larboard watch, to which I belonged, was on duty. There being no need of active labor, the sailors gathered in groups, listening to each other's yarns, many times told before, yet always interesting to those who told them, and tc those who listened, of course. The passengers had come on deck just before sunset, and still remained, forming a group on the quarter-deck, with Captain Thims and the first mate. Not having been long enough at sea to be interested in a twice-told tale, I separated from my companions, and being perhaps attracted somewhat, by the sweet Castilian *muchacha* who had so innocently entranced me, I drew near to the last-mentioned group. They were talking of the dangers of navigation. The father of my little beauty was telling a story, how, in his boyhood, he drifted out to sea with the tide in an open boat, and how, having been picked up when almost dead, by a brig, he went on a voyage of six months, returning home to his parents, who supposed him dead. This reminded Captain Thims of one similar, that had an excellent joke in it, which he rehearsed with such a hearty joviality, that we laughed until we were out of breath, and then laughed again purely on his account. We had scarcely done laughing, when the little ruddy-cheeked boy, whom I had noticed for some time back, standing a short distance apart from the company, looking intently, and rather wildly, all along the Eastern horizon, came running up to his mother, and laying his head in her lap, began to cry.

"What's the matter, my child?" inquired the mother, with much solicitude.

"My little son, what ails you?" joined in the father. "Hush! hush! I'm ashamed of you."

"What is the matter with my little boy?" again inquired the mother, feeling him shudder, as she remarked aside. But the little fellow cried on, burying his head deeper in his mother's lap.

"What ails the child? This is quite unusual," remarked the father, stepping forward to raise him up. But he clung frantically to his mother, crying as if in real despair.—"Don't let them take me—don't, mother!"

"Who? Why, my love, don't you want to come to father?"

The tender, familiar voice seemed to soothe him a little, and, looking anxiously around, he finally gave himself up to his father, in whose arms he soon fell asleep.

"Mind I tell ye there's bloody breakers ahead, or *I* never seen a capstan."

We looked around. It was an old sailor, grey

headed and scarred,—noted on board for his extreme taciturnity and dullness; and as he stood there then, his face lit up as with a flash of internal light slowly fading, a thrill of terror sent the blood from the face of every one who heard him. Captain Thims appeared peculiarly agitated, rising hurriedly and without ceremony going below. The family soon followed him, descending reluctantly and whispering among themselves. As I walked away towards the forecastle, I was somehow vaguely impressed with the idea that "the Devil"—who, being of the starboard watch, was below in his hammock, might explain the mysterious phenomena I had just witnessed. It was, however, but the passing shadow of a thought, and I joined the knot of sailors nearest at hand, listening to what was being said. I found that the circumstance of the child's fright on the quarter-deck had attracted their attention, and had given rise to stories of the most bloody and extravagant character, concerning pirates, particularly of the Sooloo pirates, in whose seas we were then sailing. I listened awhile, and then went on, visiting the other groups in succession. I found the same spirit prevailing, blood and battles being the burden of every tale. At length I grew weary and sick at the recitals, which to keep up the excitement became ridiculously extravagant, and went aft by myself alone, gazing off into the sky—now nearly overcast with heavy, swift-moving clouds—feeling very gloomy indeed. It was ten o'clock; I felt uneasy and lonely, and thirsting for some sort of social diversion, I bethought me of the helmsman, who had a few minutes before taken his post—a burly, broad-faced, good-natured fellow, to whom I owed a debt of gratitude for having once saved my life. Being near the wheelhouse, I entered noiselessly. He was standing fixedly at his post, eyeing abstractedly the huge compass before him. He did not notice me when I came in, and stood watching a minute or more before he seemed conscious of my presence. When he did, he started with a great, blank look of surprise—"Heh! lad! It's you? Is it dark out? Yes, by the gods!" he continued, looking out earnestly; "dark as the hold of a slaver. Damme! but I wish we had a moon to-night. Where's the captain, lad?"

"He is below," said I. "Went below in a hurry, some time ago—two or three hours, perhaps—and hasn't been up since."

"What's that? Ah! I mind me now. When the little boy was scart so."

"Yes," I affirmed; continuing, "that was a curious affair," and was going to say something more, when he broke in musingly, "Quite nat'ral, quite nat'ral. I've seen that same afore," and looked again abstractedly at the compass. Again I contemplated him a minute or more. He seemed unconscious of any one near him. This surprised me. Abstraction was something quite foreign to his nature; he was *always* so bright and full of heartiness and redundant humor, that I knew now something very unusual weighed upon him. While I was looking at him, getting rapidly back—in part through sympathy—to my former gloom, he raised his head slowly, and gazing rather vacantly at me, said in a low voice—"Boy that's very serious to think on. It makes me very melancholy. D'ye know, boy, we're in dangerous seas? I seen a hulk in Borneo this day week that told a tale! If ye'd a seen the blood, dark stains o' blood, boy, ye'd not stood so quietly as ye do now. Them d—d Sooloos make clean work wi' life, boy, but dirty work wi' the body o' man." After half a minute he continued,

"Will ye go below, and tell Captain Thims to come to this wheel-house directly?" As I passed along towards the companion-way to execute the order, I saw the old, grey-headed, scarred sailor scouring with desperate industry an old scimitar. He was murmuring to himself; and as I passed close by him, I caught the words, "pirates"—"morning"—"all dead." As I crept down to find the captain, I noticed that no lamp had been lit below, a thing that had never before happened within my sea-faring experience. For some foolish cause this circumstance affected me very much. I felt for the first time afraid. An undefined sense of something awful impending stole over me.

Making my way blunderingly to the captain's room, I boldly entered. He was deeply engaged with a sea-chart, and had lost all traces of agitation. I communicated the helmsman's request, mentioning his name. "Why, what ails Bill to-night?" he replied pleasantly. "He's not apt to have bugbears." He continued, rising, "I'll attend to his case. Go back to your duty." There were signs of agitation in his manner as he followed me out, which I partook of largely as I followed him along the dark way, now more light by reason of a small lantern he carried, up to the deck. Surmising that the meeting in the wheel-house would have something to do with the cause of the great fear that had fallen upon me, I approached and looked in from a little distance. They stood for some minutes in close conversation, the captain assuming a laughing indifference, the sailor evidently painfully serious. At length Captain Thims turned on his heel, and was coming out. Bill's voice took a higher pitch, and I caught the words. "Ye'd better keep him from the wheel. Now I tell ye, ye wrong us all by not doing as I tell ye."

"Shame on you, Bill," returned the captain. "You're unreasonable. That was purely accidental."

"Well, sir, ye're commander. The ship's your'n, but the lives of us all are not your'n. But you and I can't agree. It must go as you say." The captain stepped back, and patting him on the shoulder, assured him it was an idle whim, and whirling, hurriedly left the spot, yet not so quickly but that my sharpened vision detected an unusual nervousness in his step, and a pallor in his countenance. "Well,

Bill," ejaculated I with a long respiration, looking in at door.

"Boy," he answered, "come in, I want to talk to you."

I obeyed, and in a whisper he entered upon a detail of what possessed him, the substance of which was, that we were in a dangerous situation: that he had a deadly fear of 'the Devil,' heightened by the recollection of the incident at the Cape; that his trick at the wheel would come off between two and four in the morning, as he was informed; he wouldn't say just what he thought; he blamed Captain Thims; didn't know as Captain Thims could help it; and ended by wishing most heartily we had a moon. I knew his experience and his good sense, and his remarks multiplied my fears, so that I was almost afraid to leave him. But I summoned courage enough and went forward, joining the rest. They had ceased telling stories, and were ominously silent. I sought out Senk, and sitting down close to him, experienced a feeling of safety quite soothing, until he, turning suddenly upon me, said in an emphatic whisper, "Phil, I am afraid." This roused my ghastly fears to such an extent, that I believe I should have gone to my hammock against orders, hoping for relief there, had not the announcement that it was midnight given us all permission to go.

I went below with the rest and turned in. At first I could not sleep. My fears took bodily shapes. Red fires gleaming from the basements of massive buildings—creeping fires that no one could quench, making their insidious way to powder magazines; hairy, black, grim fiends in human form sneaking noiselessly along, and stabbing up beneath our hammocks; shrinking females frantically climbing the shrouds, and, pursued by the ferocious monsters, plunging from the yards into the dark sea. Thus was I assailed. Fancying that I heard something, I started up and listened. An unusual quiet prevailed. The most inveterate snorer gave not so much as a snort to remind one of his existence. Yet they were all in their berths. I heard one of them groan. I lay down again, and again my fears took bodily shapes. I was in an open boat at sea, out of sight of land. The sea was smoother than I had ever seen it before. There was not a breath of wind: so still it was, that it hardly seemed there was any atmosphere at all, and yet I was borne rapidly along, or, stationary myself, the sea moved—I knew not nor cared; something of vital and vast importance hung upon me it seemed. First, it was the pretty Castilian maiden. I tried in the dim horizon to see her. I looked, and looked until I saw her. She was in the air floating like a gossamer. She waved her hands as if keeping time to some blissful cadence. She swayed, and swam, and danced with airy leaps far before me. Now, I could not see her face. The hands were gone; no, there was one remaining. Its wavy motion was gone. It writhed. Her face turned towards me. The palor and ghastliness of death were there. It was to save her life that I was sweeping madly along. And now it was distinctly the sea that moved. The foam at the prow of my boat was gone, and I was being borne rapidly away! The white hand beckoned, beckoned—despair was in the tremor of its fingers, but I could not come.

Then I was far away. The sea narrowed—became a river narrowing. Beautiful shores smiled upon me. Then one continuous city lined them. Majestic castles; hanging-gardens watered by silvery fountains; heaven-reaching spires in endless profusion met my eye on either side; yet there was a hue of blood about it all that terrified me. The river narrowed—narrowed, became a creek. The city disappeared. I was on land, standing by a battered hulk. There were blood stains upon it, and men sweaty and worn with toil were striving to wash them off. Upon that hulk stood the form of the gigantic sailor, bearing the same expression of hot vengeance I had often seen. I beheld him awe-stricken. A sweet, soft voice in the air said "Vanish!" He smote his breast, and the blood-shot, gleaming eyes left their sockets; the long matted hair passed off in shreds upon the passing wind, and his giant bulk fell a mass of rattling bones to the ground.

Again I was in the open sea, still bent upon my mission, which grew more important as it grew more vague and objectless. My father and mother were with me. A single red light gleamed in the cloudy sky. It became brighter and brighter. It was the face of the beautiful bride. She smiled upon us, and waved her hand away as if to some distant land whither she was going, and a clear, angelic voice came over the sea—"I am on earth no more,"—"No more," was the soft echo that sank sleeping upon the distant waves.

I turned around. My father and mother were gone. The sea and cloudy sky were gone. I was upon a mountain top—upon a crag that overhung a beautiful valley far, far down. In that valley were men struggling in mortal combat. Among them was Captain Thims, armed to the teeth. I saw him fall. A bloody knife grasped by a giant hand—a bloody face flashed in the sun. It was a face that I knew—the face of the grim sailor. "You are a murderer," I shouted. In deafening tones my voice pealed down the mountain side. A thousand echoes caught it up, and rung it far, far away, until the earth shook as with the roll of distant thunder. Hark! It has become suddenly still—dark and still. A hand is on mine. I start as though stung by a serpent.

"What! boy, ye afraid?" Pshaw! I had been sleeping. "Bill," said I in a whisper, for he whispered, "did it thunder just now?"

"No. I guess ye must a-heard 'the Devil' taking his place at the wheel. It has been mighty still otherwise, I tell ye. Boy, I do wish 'twas morning. Boy, I have a plan. Senk and me has been talking it over. We can't neither of us sleep, and we're going slily on deck, to watch a little, you know. Wouldn't ye go along?" "Yes, lad," put in Senk, hoarsely whispering, "come along." I needed no urging. We went together on deck, taking up our position on the forecastle. Senk, experienced and sagacious, noticed at once, that the wind was from a new quarter. He communicated the fact to Bill, who thought it very singular, as we were still on the same tack he knew. The wind was directly astern. Possibly it had changed. Nothing more was said on the subject for a while. Senk had had a dream, very extravagant, very disastrous. He told it to us elaborately in a whisper, which became subvocal at emphatic passages. Then I told mine. Between the two dreams, nearly an hour passed. After my dream was told, we were silent. "It's strange Mr. Dory don't notice this change in the wind. He must be asleep," remarked Senk. "It is strange," replied Bill, and there was silence again. The weight of the night began to show itself upon Senk. He was nodding; and a peculiar indifference was creeping upon me, when a whisper—with a deep ominous tone which stopped my heart dead still for an instant—said, "We're off our course, or the north star has changed place." I looked in the direction Bill's finger was pointing. A rent in the clouds showed a patch of sky. There it was, the north star right off astern. At the same time there was a movement on the quarter. "What are you about there at the wheel, asleep?" shouted the mate, and then proceeded to order a put about, concluding with a hope that he at the helm, would keep awake. "Ay, ay, sir!"—wide awake enough, we thought. The clouds closed again.—Had an angel opened them that we might see?—Still the wind continued from the same quarter. "Passing strange Mr. Dory don't notice it," reflected Senk. But Mr. Dory was a dull, amiable man, and did not notice it. "Captain Thims must know this" said Bill, agitated, though determined; "and I'll go and tell him now." We had no objection, and he started. Just as he reached the companion-way he was hailed by Mr. Dory. "Halloa! larboard, what you doing here?" Then followed a silence, broken to Senk and me by Bill and Mr. Dory coming forward in close, subdued conversation. I was listening, when Senk laid his hand, which trembled, upon my arm, and speaking aloud, told me to look forward, out on the sea. Far out on the distant horizon, directly in our course, I saw a blood-red light—small yet distinct—like the single red light of my dream. Mr. Dory saw it, Bill saw it, and we stood looking intently at it for half a minute, perhaps when it disappeared.

"Peace, and good will to men, I say; for the kingdom of Heaven is at hand to some of us, that's fixed," commented Senk.

"I believe you, Bill," said Mr. Dory. "We have a traitor here. Do you keep watch here, and I'll attend to him." Summoning half a dozen men to his assistance, Mr. Dory proceeded without noise to the wheelhouse. I attended them. We halted near, where we could distinctly see the object of our suspicions. His strong hands were firm on the wheel, his dark, lowering gaze fiercely directed towards the point where the light had appeared. The mate entered and touched his shoulder. He started, yet seeing who it was, sneered most scornfully, and turned away. "Where are you driving us to?" firmly demanded Mr. Dory. "To H—l," was the contemptuous reply. "Well, sir, you can leave this wheel,—the sooner the better." "Have you orders from the captain?" coolly inquired the other.

"That happens to be none of your business," retorted the mate.

"Well, sir, I shan't *leave* without orders from him."

"We'll help you," quietly responded Mr. Dory, and ordered the men to arrest him. This was achieved through much struggling, and hard words, and the giant was carried below.

Another man was appointed to the wheel; the light at the prow was extinguished, and the one in the wheel-house carefully screened. Our course was resumed, bearing away from the portentous light, which had again appeared, larger, apparently nearer.

"Where is the second mate of this vessel?" sounded harshly through the darkness. It was the voice of Captain Thims, scarcely recognizable for its hoarseness and depth. There was no answer. "Is any one at the wheel?" he demanded, walking that way. No answer. Coming to the wheel-house, he said with a fierceness strange indeed for him, addressing the helmsman, "Scoundrel! I'll stab you to death if you don't tell me what this means this instant. I'll not be fooled with this way. Where's the second mate?

tell me, d—n you! quick, or I'll blow out your brains." The man, frightened at the dreadful anger which possessed the Captain, confusedly told him the state of things.

"Poor devil!" ejaculated Captain Thims, "he don't know what he has done. Where is he—the mate?"

"Look yonder, will you," said the mate, now at his side, and pointing to the light. Captain Thims looked; but the light had disappeared, and he saw it not. "Do you know what you are about, you rascal?" said he to Mr. Dory. "Recall that man instantly, and put him at the wheel."

"I beg of you, Captain Thims, to consider"——

"Not one word, sir, if you will not drive me to extremities," interrupted the captain, making a gesture towards the pistol in his breast pocket. Astounded at the unaccountable conduct of Captain Thims, the mate recalled 'the Devil,' and placed him at the wheel. This done, he suggested to Captain Thims the necessity of arming the crew. "All fudge," sneered the captain. "If you are afraid, go below, the whole of you. I'll take charge of the vessel till morning."

Though this was said in an ironical manner, we took him at his word by common consent, and went below. The larboard watch were apprised of what was going on, and getting up, we all proceeded to the armory, where each procured a weapon. The first mate proposed going on deck. But Mr. Dory, knowing the consequences, dissuaded him. "A few minutes more, and we shall be called on deck! I fear resistance will be vain. This is to my mind but the consummation of a deep plot, which so far has had no hindrance. I do not implicate Captain Thims; but I do think he is deceived—or perhaps he can't help it. His conduct is strange, unaccountable. But let us fight like men. The case is by no means hopeless." Thus talked Mr. Dory in a whisper, the last two remarks being spoken aloud. Then Mr. Remy, the first mate, offered some remarks. He was yet speaking when the sharp report of a pistol was heard, and the sound of quick, heavy footsteps overhead. "On, men! Follow me!" shouted Mr. Dory, unsheathing his sword, and rushing up the companion-way. Desperately we struggled up. Three succeeded in reaching the deck. Establishing a footing there, they guarded the advent of those behind. I was the fifth. For an instant I was appalled. Throngs of black, ugly fiends were pouring over the bulwarks and making for the hatchway. Despair made me brave, and I sprang upon the deck. I had just time to see the reeling form of Captain Thims swaying towards us, the target of a dozen pikes, when a strong blow laid me senseless.

I must have remained in that condition several hours. When I recovered consciousness the deck was deserted. All was still about the ship. It was broad daylight. I arose with difficulty and looked around. The first object of which I got a distinct idea, was the dead body of Mr. Dory. I thought I heard a noise in the wheel-house. I went there, hoping to find some one alive. It was the breathing of the giant sailor had attracted me. He was lying on his back, a loathsome object. His eyes and nose had been shot away, apparently by a close discharge. Did Captain Thims do this? and was that first report the one? So I thought, as I turned away. Dead bodies were lying thickly all around. The conflict had been bravely sustained. Senk—the good Senk—was among the dead; and Bill, too, and Captain Thims, the first mate, and many more. I found and recognized them one by one. Yet they were not all there. The strife must have been continued below, thought I, and approached the hatchway for the purpose of descending. Suddenly I heard steps and strange sounds below. They approached. What could I do? Flight was absurd. I had, then, been left for dead. The fiends were yet on board. Fear chained me to the spot. In a few moments a huge, flat, bushy head, with small tiger eyes, thick, pug nose, and monstrous mouth, showed itself. It contemplated me for a short space, with a greedy grin. Another moment and I was in a grasp of iron. My hands and feet were quickly tied, and I was laid on my back to await the caprice of my captor.

From my position I could not see what was going on; but from what I could hear, I concluded the savages were plundering the ship at their leisure. I lay perhaps an hour, when my captor came, and taking me up as he would have taken up a bundle of merchandise, handed me down the side of the ship to his comrades, who stowed me away among some boxes and trunks, and left me to myself.

Imagining death could not be very immediate, I gradually gave way to the stupor which sought possession of me, and fell asleep. The effects of several causes conspired to plunge me into a deep, dreamless slumber, in which I remained till late in the afternoon. I awoke to find myself aboard of a large, rough-hewn, sort of an ancient galley. It had one sail, an irregular shaped sheet, intended for square, and it was steered by means of a long oar. There were five other large boats like the one I was on, besides several small craft manned by six to twelve men each. Their course seemed to be southeast. On board the concern which carried me, I counted thirty men—all huge and muscular, apparently picked. There was no deck—only a kind of cabin in the afterpart, in which the master sat enthroned like a monarch:—indeed, he was king, as it afterwards appeared,—chieftain of the whole swarm. I was on board the admiral!

My bonds having been removed during my sleep, I was free to walk, and scrutinize as inclination directed. After forming an idea of my general situation, I followed up my investigations, and became quite interested in the phenomena transpiring around me. The hideous forms of the beings that peopled the squadron all looked pretty much alike, differing only in degrees of hideousness. Their motions were awkward, and clumsy like black bears', and sly:—everything was done second-handed. If one wished to pick his nose, for instance, he would put up his hand and scratch the backside of his head, and then slide his hand clandestinely forward under his chin, and so on, up to his nose, dabbing it a little, and finally making a gesture with the hand to cover the manœuvre. Their language was inexpressible, at least it seemed so literally. Of all the lingual incongruities that made Babel a tower of nonsense, I think this must have been the most unconformable. The act of speech to them was apparently an act of partial strangulation, into which they were perseveringly plunging and recovering from doubtfully, to the great distortion of the countenance and of the whole body. If an orator had existed among them, I think the effect of his elocution must have depended upon his actual death by strangulation, and a syncope of the auditory through giving applause.

After amusing myself for a time with contemplating and comparing, I became sensible of a great hunger prowling within. I approached my captor, whom I knew by a deep scar in his forehead, and asked him for food, as well as I could by signs. Disguising the act with a feint or two, he furtively drew forth from a bag which hung before him, a piece of dried meat, and gave me. In my hunger I ate voraciously, not noticing until I came to the last morsel that it had a texture and flavor entirely new; and I did not stop to think of it then, but asked him for more. He lifted up the leopard-skin robe that was slung loosely over him, and displaying his brawny thigh, made a carving motion upon it, and shook the empty bag. How was I to understand this? To signify he had no more, shaking the bag would have been sufficient. Why carve his thigh in that imaginary way? The idea must not be harbored. I should starve. I walked away. But the idea clung to me like a repulsive odor; it impregnated me like a drug, deeper and deeper. Dizzy, nauseated, I went to the side of the boat, and there my stomach promptly performed its disagreeable function. I was freed, and thankful. Human flesh! Could a Christian conscience, much less a Christian stomach, bear such aliment? I chose starvation rather.

Quietly and beamingly the day passed on its western journey: sadly and quietly the night closed in. As the last soft flush of evening twilight melted from the skirts of night, a sea-bird went wailing into the far west. The sound was so mournful that even the grim savages looked after it, and at each other, soberly. Oh! how unexpressibly mournful it was to me! The novelty of my situation had diverted me from recalling the horrors of the past night. Now they came back, overwhelming me as a tide. Could I have wept, could I have sighed, it might have eased my heart; but sighs and tears were a mockery. I felt suffocated with the burden. I thought of the sweet picture upon which my soul had feasted the evening before; of the little boy's fright; of the old sailor's prophecy; of my dream, and the smiling face of the beautiful bride as she waved her lily hand, and of her prophetic words; of the brave men rushing to the deck, and I strove to imagine the terrific struggle for life upon that deck, slippery with blood; of the descent of the frightful fiends, after finishing their sanguine work above. There my mind stopped; I could not think of what followed; but the vague impression dwelt upon me, saddening me almost to a swoon. I grew faint and stupid, and sinking down among the boxes, I fell into another deep sleep. I slept soundly until morning, waking, as the day broke, to a dream of home. I was yet in the midst of it, when the sun's rays flashing over the sea, drove the soothing visitant from me.

As the morning advanced, I happily made a discovery of a chest of Christian food, which had been preserved as a curiosity I suppose, and amused the crew by eating a long time unreservedly therefrom. My breakfast refreshed me so much that I felt quite resigned to my dubious state. The day passed dismally and monotonously, and another night came on. A brisk northwest breeze set in at sunset, blowing steadily until near midnight. Towards morning a heavy storm passed far to the south, flashing and thundering grandly, and by daylight the sea around us ran pretty high. One of the boats capsized, unloading itself very promiscuously. The living part of the cargo was saved, but the balance was lost. The sea, however, grew calm after a short time, and the northwest breeze rising again, the squadron went on its way.

About three o'clock we hove in sight of land. A large, red flag was immediately run up from the admiral, and in a few minutes a like signal appeared on the distant shore; whereupon a general strangu-

'ation took place, ultimating in a deep howl that was awful to listen to.

Just before sunset we came to land, a most dreary-looking beach, opening up into an uneven, sterile prospect. About twenty beasts of burden, little larger than good-sized dogs, stood ranged, tails seaward, waiting for booty. While the vessels were being unloaded, I saw one package which, from their handling it very carefully, attracted my attention. It was a long wicker basket covered with white cloth. My curiosity was strangely excited, and being on shore I determined to know what it was. So I walked directly to it, and putting my hand upon the top, presently discovered it to contain something living. Oh, my heart! how it leapt! I conjectured the truth, Hastily tearing the screen away, I saw, pale and emaciated, yet conscious, the little Spanish maiden, dearest of all whom I had supposed dead. She recognized me at once, and smiled, putting up her hand as though to greet me. I took it, overwhelmed with the tenderest emotions.

"Is there none but you?" she asked feebly. I shook my head, pressing the dear little hand fervently.

"Will they kill us?" she asked apprehensively.

"I don't know," I replied. "If they do we will die together."

She pressed my hand now in turn, and raised her head a little, as though to kiss me, or for me to kiss her. I did not stop to inquire, but getting down on my knees, pressed my lips to hers, dizzy with emotion. Then I lifted her out of her cradle, as I would have lifted a babe, tenderly assisting her to her feet, and she stood leaning upon my arm. On her expressing a desire to walk, we proceeded together a short distance along the beach. As we walked, she told me that she had occupied that basket ever since the morning which had risen upon that fearful night, partaking of food but once, though they had offered it to her many times; she could not eat, she was so very sad, thinking of her father and mother, and little brother gone. As we were returning she asked my name. I told her.

"Anne is my English name," she said. "You shall be my brother, Philip, while we live. If they don't kill us, we will run away from these ugly men some day, and go home to Borneo, and you shall live with me, and we will live together for ever." Poor sailor boy! Without protection amidst a horde of cannibals, and with so little power to protect, what a charge was his! I have often in solitary moments recalled the feelings of that night, and wondered at the manliness with which I bore up against despair.

After unloading their boats, the savages, except four, returned to them, and drifted off with the tide just ebbing. The four who remained fell assisting the drivers, and before it was entirely dark the beasts of burden were packed and ready for departure. They deliberated some time concerning us. Finally they took the wicker basket, and strapping it ingeniously to one of the animals, lifted Anne up carefully, and placed her in it. Then putting the rope, which was around the beast's neck, in my hand, bade me by signs to lead on, which I did most willingly.

The guide, or director, went a short space ahead, and the whole cavalcade followed slowly.

About midnight we entered a low dense thicket, through which we groped for some time, coming out at last right upon a little huddle of rude tents, which looked very white in the clear moonlight. There were twenty-five, perhaps thirty of them—

close together, the openings for entrance occurring in every possible relative position to each other.

Here we halted. About a score of women, and as many children, were immediately present, coming from nowhere that I could see, and joined eagerly in unpacking and lugging off the booty. While this was going on, I helped Anne to dismount. I had hardly accomplished it when we were closely thronged with a new swarm of children. They seemed to stand in no sort of awe, but were on the contrary most impudently curious—investigating our persons very annoyingly. This we resisted gently at first. They grew furious; and one of them, a squatty, dwarfish-looking thing, struck Anne a hard blow on her arm. Regardless of what the consequences might be, I returned the blow with all the force I could muster, and it was a hard one, I assure you. The little imp turned a complete summersault, and lay stretched out senseless. This summary act seemed to terrify the rest, and they disappeared like shadows. The next visitation was the women. Having discharged their manual duties, they came around us, and at once entered upon an examination. One felt my arms and legs, and taking my hand, pinched up the ball of my thumb and the flesh on the side. Then looking around at her companions, she made a motion of carving the flesh off. One of them, who seemed to be very old, and whose face I saw clearly by the moonlight, responded to the motion with a grin, while the saliva drivelled out of her mouth.

I was glad they saw no such enticement in Anne, and I was also glad to see that Anne did not apprehend the import of what was going on.

The examination, afterwards more desultory, continued for some time. When it was done, we were led around through various windings, through two or three tents, until we came to one lower and more oblong than the rest. Into this we were pushed, and the opening carefully folded after us. In the middle of the tent, on the ground, resting in an iron mortar, was a large spermaceti candle burning. By the light of this, we discovered two piles of blankets, one in each end of the tent, and the chest of food from which I had fed while on board the boat. After partaking from the chest, we retired to forget in sleep for a few hours, the terrors with which we were surrounded.

I awoke at day-break; but Anne slept on quietly, and I sat by her watching her slumbers. As I sat looking upon her placid face, my mind recurred to our situation, and I speculated by turns hopefully and despondingly, upon our immediate destiny. I thought not much, and cared less about myself. The sweet creature before me was my care. They would kill us no doubt, thought I,—murder us as cannibals ever murder their victims. But I knew what cannibals were. I knew they would not kill us then—that day, nor that week; perhaps not for months. We were not then fit for their worse than hellish repast. We might get away from them. If not, I might persuade them to spare Anne, and deliver her up to her friends, representing to them the certainty of their reaping thereby large sums of gold. I should have learned their language, so as to tell them this. Thus thinking and planning, I sat watching her as she slept. After a while her sleep was less quiet. A vivid dream seemed to possess her. She smiled. Her eyelids quivered as with joy. She made a blind motion with her hand, stroking tenderly the rough blanket, and smiled again, while tears oozed forth, gathering in little drops upon her long eyelashes.

Then a deep shadow of sadness suddenly darkened every feature, and she was awake. "O, Philip! is he gone?" she exclaimed in a tone of deepest anguish.

"Who?" I asked, almost weeping from sympathy, so wildly pathetic was her tone and manner.

"Dear little brother. Oh, what a sweet dream I have had!" she continued, relapsing into the memory of it. "I cannot tell it to you. So pretty he looked standing by me. He would not stay. But he went away quickly, as I have heard my mother say angels fly away, up towards the sky, so quick I did not see where he went. Is it morning, Philip?"

I assured her it was, and directly brought her something to eat.

She ate a little, and then putting the unfinished morsel back into my hand, and covering her face, she began to weep most bitterly. I soothed her as well as I could, asking her again and again why she wept. When she had recovered her voice, she told me that at the evening meal before that awful night, she had shared just such a cake with her little brother. Soon she became quite calm. Yet the incident had taken her back to those dreadful scenes, and from a melancholy interest in them, I suppose, she asked me to narrate what happened to me after they went below to retire. This I did, as near as my emotions would allow. When I had finished, I in turn asked her to tell what befell her. "O, Philip, how can I tell you? It is so dreadful," she began, shuddering. "But I will tell you, if I can," she continued after a pause. "I was asleep with little brother, and mother and father in one room. In another, with a door between, was sister and Carlos. When I awoke, father was holding the door: mother was helping him. I was frightened, and began to cry. My sister then came in, and a little while after, Carlos went to help father. He said they had done trying to get in at his door, and were all trying to get in there. My sister came to me, and put her arms around me, and told me we had all to die that night, and told me to look for her when I would be in the spirit world. I heard dreadful noises outside,—men swearing, and saying they were killed; and snarling noises like tigers and lions fighting together. Sister looked so pale I was afraid of her. Little brother awoke and cried just as he did that evening. He cried just as he did then—'Don't let them take me, mother.' I began to feel brave when little brother cried, and I tried to hush him. Carlos went into the other room for his sword. When he came back, he told sister that the crew seemed to be all dead, and now he and father must fight. He went to the door again. I heard a loud noise like a gun outside, and father let go of the door and fell back. Mother caught hold of him, so that he did not quite fall down; but he could not stand up, and mother and sister helped him to the bed and he lay down. He was very pale, and he put both hands on his breast, and gasped very hard. I went up to the bed. Mother and sister were bending over him and crying. I put my arms around him. He said, 'O my God!' in Spanish, and breathed a long breath. My mother and sister cried louder, and said he was dead. I put my face upon his hand and cried, too. The noise outside came so much louder, that I looked up. The door was open, and Carlos was standing before it, striking as hard as he could with his sword at the awful looking men that were trying to get in. A monstrous man fell into the room, dead. The head of another one tumbled over Carlos' shoulder upon the floor. Mother, sister, and brother and I went into sister's room. My mother put her arms around little brother and me, and sat down in one corner. Sister walked the room, wringing her hands, and saying in Spanish, 'O! my husband! They will kill him. They will kill him. O! mother, what shall I do?' Then she tried to go out and help Carlos. My mother would not let her. While they were struggling, my sister tried hard to go. I heard another sound like a gun, and Carlos came running in, and tried to shut the door after him. But a very large black man—I saw the same man last night—pressed close in after him, and they grappled with each other. The last I remember, they were struggling dreadfully.

When I came to myself, I was tied and lying on the floor. I could not stir. No one was near me as I could see, and so I did not cry for help, but lay there a long time very still. When I was almost exhausted, lying there so still, those frightful black men came and took me up. As they were carrying me out, I saw Carlos lying in sister's arms. They were deadly pale, and their clothes bloody. I think they were both dead.—Oh, it makes me feel so lonely now to think of it! I was afraid of the black men, and did not feel so then. I did not see mother, nor little brother.—Oh, I am so lonely, Philip. "Why do you weep, Philip? It is past now. I shall not cry any more." She sat up, and twined her fingers in my hair, begging me not to weep. But I could not help it.—So sad a tale! and to my ear so sweetly told!

It was nearly noon. She arose, and we went together to the chest and partook of food. She ate quite plentifully, and declared herself much renewed, desiring to walk out. This we did. To our great surprise, we saw no one. The village seemed wholly deserted. Satisfied, from careful examination, that it was really so, a plan presented itself immediately to my mind, and I determined to carry it directly into execution. I proposed it to Anne. Her judgment agreed with mine. We would make our escape! In a few minutes we were ready, having packed some food in a small bag which we found amongst the rubbish of the tent.

We struck directly into the thicket, and made for the sea-shore, whence we had come. We travelled slowly all that afternoon, neither seeing nor hearing anything of our captors. Resting a little at sunset, and taking some food, we travelled on until midnight. Anne had borne up under the fatigue remarkably but now her tottering step and laborious breathing admonished me of the necessity of repose. So, looking out a sheltered place—it was a small cave in the side of a hill—I smoothed a little space, and, sitting down, took her in my arms, placing her head upon my bosom. She was soon asleep, and I sat thus holding her until morning. She awoke greatly refreshed, and we went on our way. We had not gone far when we came in sight of the sea. A great difficulty upon which I had not counted, now presented itself. The sea would put an end to our path. We had no boat. "Perhaps we shall find one on the beach," said Anne. Perhaps. We would try. We soon arrived at the water's edge. No boat could we see. We walked along the beach a mile or more. Still no boat. I found an oar. As we walked on, almost despairing, Anne stumbled. What was it? It looked like a keel. It was one. With my oar I dug away the sand and pebbles. It was a boat buried in the sand. With considerable labor I removed it, and launched it. We consigned ourselves to it, floating slowly out upon the deep. There was a gentle breeze seaward, and making a mast of my oar, and a sail of my jacket, we drifted quite rapidly and pleasantly far out, losing sight of land before night. When it was entirely dark I took down the sail, and making as comfortable a place as I could for Anne, I watched her and the sea, while she slept. I watched awhile, and then fell asleep myself. Neither of us awoke until daybreak, and then both awoke together, to give forth a shout of rapturous joy. We were but a short distance away from a ship, and within speaking distance of a boat which had been sent out to pick us up. We were shortly on board. It was an American vessel, hailing from Boston, and homeward bound. Anne wanted to get off at Borneo, but unfavorable winds bore us far to the northward of that port, and it was deemed impracticable to put back. She went with me to Boston. The captain of the ship, a benevolent man, took a deep and friendly interest in her, and took her to his own house. I engaged myself in his service, and wrote to my parents. Before leaving port, I had the great happiness of seeing my father and mother, and of consigning my orphan charge to them. What became of her afterwards, as well as what befell me, would double the length of my story to relate. I will not enter upon it. When I began, I thought I would tell you all about my experience as a sailor; but it is getting quite late, and I must quit here in the middle,—fully conscious, by the by, that I have discharged my obligation in the way of story-telling. However, I cannot leave it without stating, that the little Spanish maiden became one day a wife, and the sailor boy a husband, and—father.

CHAPTER V.

It was bed-time, late bed-time, after midnight, when the supposed lawyer brought his narration to a close. A general stretching and yawning immediately ensued, accompanied with a casual consultation of watches, and sundry mingled allusions to some of the incidents of the story, and to the necessity of sleep. Our lean friend of the bar had yielded to that necessity, as we discovered on approaching for lights, and was, as it seemed, laboring with vile imaginings of a piratical or other bloody character. His countenance bore an expression of great horror, which with the slight, yet significant motions of his hands, indicated that he was desperately resisting some awful bugbear or other. The Quaker touched him with his cane. He exploded with a wild shout of terror that awoke him at once, and completely.

"You should go better armed, my dear fellow," remarked the Quaker. He made no reply, being evidently offended at our merriment, and hastening to comply with our demand for lights, directed us in a general way to our places of repose, whither we retired to dream or reflect, or both in one, as the mind's tone chanced to be.

How the rest of the company enjoyed the night I do not know. My sleep was very calm, I remember; and the cold grey morning came quite too soon for me. The morning was indeed cold and grey. The sun, judging from appearances, did not rise at all—only sending a delegation of light, which like delegations generally, seemed to have mostly forgotten the purpose of its sending. A kind of dense mist that was not quite rain, but if anything wetter than rain, filled all the nether atmosphere. There was a cold, north wind, too, a wind such as causes the mercury in old men's bones to sink gratingly. It blew with a whistling sound, around the old building, and roared away most gloomily, like flying ghosts, through the stinted forest which bordered a neighboring stream.

The transition from the warm bed to my ungenial pantaloons was so disagreeable that it put me quite out of humor, and looking out at the little four-paned window of my apartment, to assure myself that I had not been dreaming about the weather, I took an oath, which was an oath, not to continue my journey *that* day.

As we sat at the breakfast table, I overheard the two farmer-like looking men say one to the other, by way of exchange of remarks, that they should not go on until the sky cleared. This was a comfort. I should not be all alone. "Do you think of sallying out to-day, sir," inquired the Quaker of me. I answered emphatically in the negative, alluding to my oath.

"Quite singular!—the coincidence, I mean," he said in reply; "I pledged *my*self between the bed and my pantaloons this morning to the same effect."

"Well, I've taken no vow on the subject," remarked the lawyer, supposed to be, "but I think I shall try the effect of this latitude and longitude a little before going on. I'm in no hurry if the rest are not, I'm sure."

"This looks like staying," said the grey-headed man, laughing. "So it does," gushingly responded the lawyer, partly in answer to the old man's laugh.

"I believe I know what you want to stay for, too," said the grey-headed, further, with another laugh.

"Eh, you do?" poured out the lawyer again, amused at the old man's laughable hilarity. "Yes. It's to hear them 'ere men's stories there," pointing to the Quaker and me. This remark seemed very aptly put in, evidently touching the secret inclinations of all, for the subject was immediately dropped, and no more brought up that day.

After breakfast it occurred to me to suggest a reorganization for the purpose of continuing the entertainment. I did so while cigars were being lit. "By no means; by-no-means," responded the lawyer. "In such a case we should have the day pleasantly passed it is true; but the night cometh, you know. That would hang, and hang us with it I'm afraid. Be prudent my dear sir. Remember the foolish virgins. What do you say my friend?" addressing the Quaker.

"I will fall in with the majority when there shall be one," replied the other. "Well, that's fair, spoken like a man, a true republican," continued the lawyer, "and my point is carried, for I'm a majority in myself!"

I succumbed, and formally withdrew my proposition, with reluctance, however, not exactly seeing the force of the lawyer's logic, and being impatient to hear what the Quaker might have for us. "But how are you going to pass the day?" I asked by way of covering my retreat.

"Pass it if you can; if you can't, let it pass you,—it will be all the same. I intend to follow this advice, brother, and can conscientiously offer it. Moreover, what I say unto you, I say unto all. I have spoken." Delivering himself of this facetiousness, the lawyer strode out to take a view of the weather. He directly returned, full of animation, declaring he had a new idea, a return of an old want, which he had looked upon as among things past to come back no more, namely, a desire to go a-fishing. "And now," he concluded, "will any one go along?" No one seemed so much disposed to join him as the Quaker, and out of politeness none of the rest of us offered. They were soon in readiness, two oilcloth overalls, and fishing tackle being raised, and started off full of mock anticipation and glee.

The two farmers fell into a pleasant vein of informing each other of the promising prospects of the live stock trade; of the best manner of procuring as well as of curing said stock; of the celebrated standard male progenitors in the cattle line, in the horse line, and so on and so forth, much varied, and with great relish. The jolly old man listened, became interested by degrees, and joined in the conversation. I listened, and lost interest in about the same ratio that he gained it, and finally went to my room. I ordered a comfortable fire to be built, and taking pencil and paper, amused myself with sketching down, as nearly as I could remember, the two stories of the past evening. Busied with this, the day passed so pleasantly away, that I forgot my dinner totally, and was surprised into a consciousness of the fact by the unmistakable approach of night. I went down stairs, and into the bar-room, just in time to receive the fishers. "We have not escaped the proverbial fisherman's luck," cheerfully announced the Quaker.

"No sir," confirmed the lawyer, emphatically. "However, we have something more than local saturation. Look here, will ye?" They were both dripping wet. "No fault of ours, however, let it be inserted," continued the lawyer.

"But of that great fish, eh?" suggested the Quaker, comically.

"Of that great fish," returned the other. The Quaker laughed heartily; and, as soon as he could be heard, the lawyer related the circumstance. They were both on a log at the time—a log, one end of which floated in the stream. At one and the same instant their hooks caught, or something caught the hooks—the latter it seemed was the supposition of the lawyer—and pulling hard and enthusiastically, they were both drawn, as the lawyer asserted, into the water. Fortunately it proved to be only neck-deep, and they succeeded in getting out, and in recovering their fishing poles. The hooks, though, remained fast, and they continued pulling until at last both hooks broke, and they were compelled to desist. We were yet laughing at the incident and the lawyer when supper was made known. Waiting only so long as was necessary for our wet friends to change their garments, we proceeded in a body to the passive table, and demonstrated our carnality in a most vigorous manner, and with agreeable results, for the space of half an hour or so. Just as I began to see clearly through the operation, having fixed my eye and mind upon the morsels I would eat and no more, the fact came to me, that I might soon be standing, or more probably sitting, before the present company in the character of social entertainer.

It was a serious thing, more so as I was disagreeably conscious of sore deficiency. The consideration threw me into a fit of absence, which directly attracted the lawyer's attention.

"You men take it to heart very much, don't you?" he said, rallyingly. I looked around. The Quaker was smiling assent. He, too, had been absent.

"What do you mean?" said I, with assumed innocence.

"Oho! what do you mean!" laughingly retorted the other. "You've no idea of getting out of it I hope. Hang your pluck, if you do. Here we've been waiting all day, so our venerable friend here asserts, and probably believes, for the sole purpose of having our fun out, and now we"——

"Oh, I apprehend your allusion now," said I, coming out of my hypocrisy; "you touch upon the matter of story-telling. Don't be frightened, sir. The heaven is *not* falling. But bear in mind *I* ought to be excused, for I wanted the thing to go along in the morning, and you opposed."

"Opposed on good grounds, sir, as will presently be, if it has not already been, disclosed unto you." And so the subject was dropped.

Supper being satisfactorily concluded, we adjourned to the bar-room, to undergo a general surprise at the change which had suddenly taken place in the weather. The sun had just set, smiling a resplendent twilight over all the western heavens, while the dismal clouds were folding themselves away into the southeast, looking intensely black. From the south came a soft breeze, mild, like an infant's breath, and fragrant—most gratefully fragrant and genial—renewing life and thought—old life and old thought, thought that came of memories, tender as the wind itself, and floating like that in sweet gushes from a sunny zone!

The porch was on the south side of the house, and we were all standing there silently contemplating and enjoying, when our lean attendant drew our attention by approaching with four chairs and arranging them. Under the circumstances we needed no plainer suggestion, and, waiting politely until two more chairs were added, which the emaciated speedly brought, we sat down without reserve, continuing silent the while—a meditative mood prevailing.

The glowing twilight became less glowing, fading slowly and serenely, and the evening star came out in its midst, a living gem upon its bosom. Then it grew fainter, and the cheerful star grew brighter, —brighter, like hope in death. The moon began to cast faint shadows from earthly objects, silvering the wet leaves of the trees and bushes, silvering the fences, and barn roof, and the hay-stacks in the distant meadow, all the while looking down with its honest, half-bandaged countenance, a very saint of benevolence.

The twilight was nearly gone. The evening star was setting. The moon was in its glory. The soft south-wind blew yet soothingly, and wafting fragrance as of many flowers, when the lawyer, rising with great gravity, announced that the hour had arrived, yea, the minute, which he intended to celebrate by requiring a continuance of the last night's entertainment. "It becomes then my painful necessity to renew my staff of office. I wish it to be considered therefore, that I am duly in the chair—or shall be in a moment—and—let us have a motion." Eager to escape the ordeal for the present,

I promptly motioned that the Quaker be appointed. In due form the motion was carried, and the Quaker declared chosen. Upon which we arranged ourselves the better to listen, and sat waiting in the most profound silence for what might come forth.

CHAPTER VI.

You are undoubtedly aware,—thus the Quaker began, while we were eagerly listening,—that it is embarrassing for one to attempt the keeping up of an entertainment of this kind. You are aware that a good joke rarely brooks a companion, even of the same order; that a fine touch of sentiment goes over the heart complete in itself, and would lose its singleness and come short of its proper depth of effect by the intrusion of another, however fine. To feel the last, finest vibration of a tone of music, it must go on undisturbed. To feel the last, deepest tremor of senti ment in the centre of our being—that tremor which angels in sympathy catch, and breathe back a wave of bliss that is of heaven—there must be no intrusion. I make these remarks in view of the passages from the soul uttered here last night. I make them, too, partly in view of the genial circumstances that have sur rounded us for the last hour, speaking to us mysteriously of other times and scenes, of other hopes and joys; for I fear my voice will be a discord, the images which my words will present, unwelcome to you. Indeed it is embarrassing, though I have no doubt you will be lenient.

When this matter was suggested last evening, I had no idea, as I suppose none of you had, that it would take such a turn as it has. And again, in view of the necessity of continuing in the same strain that has characterized the entertainment thus far, I feel a hesitancy. The others have made their own life the theme. I must do so too; or, being altogether inexperienced in weaving fiction, my narrative will be a wretched mockery. It is compelling one to straits disagreeable, and yet agreëable, too, withal. However, I will not tire you with more extended preface. My story will be long and tame at best, as it now appears to my mind, and the sooner I enter, the sooner, relatively speaking, I shall get out.

I have said I should have to draw upon my own experience, chiefly for want of other. I will commence with my boyhood as the most convenient point, and continue until—elaboration shall have ceased to be a virtue, if you please. I will discreetly confine myself to the region of memory, going no further back than I can vouch for with an unsullied conscience, which is to the age when my boyhood began. I was called Deacon, and happily was the nickname conceived, if we may link the primitive association with that word; for no antiquated family cow, ruminating in the abundant shade at summer noon-tide, was ever less designing than I. The impulse of the heart was not always spoken, it is true; but when speech or action did make manifest the goings on within, it was with utter singleness—unequivocal straightforwardness. I never told a lie, I think, during the whole of my long boyhood—except once, and then it was concerning a little girl about whom I was very much bored. This little girl kissed me once, and some one saw it done, and afterwards asked me about it. I denied it point blank, and stuck faithfully to the denial. This lie my conscience never has disturbed, and I doubt whether it could anywhere be found in the Book of Human Discrepancies. They called me Deacon so much, and so seldom mentioned my proper name, that I fell into the way of thinking I had no other, and used to tell inquiring strangers, with the utmost sincerity, and much to their amusement, that my name was Deacon Munn. Yet I had another nickname. It was "Hashy." One cheerful little being always called me Hashy. It was the little girl whom I have alluded to. A sweet, lovely creature she was—that little girl;—always happy when those around her were so, and sad, tearful, when those she loved—and they were everybody—were sorrowful. She was my daily companion during those early days. When I was not at her house, she was at mine, coming always in the afternoon, soon after dinner, with the ever-glad announcement on her tongue, that her "ma" had said she might stay till the short clock pointer was on the figure V. She used to play with me in the house when it was winter; and in the spring we used to wander out together, away down into the old meadow, where there was a brook, a clear, pebbly-bottomed stream, that made mysterious music in its flow. There we would sit for hours upon the bank, talking and making nosegays; and when we were tired, we used to listen to the low, strange music which the brook made, until we were sad, and felt a dim sense of awe creeping upon us. Ay, our souls felt a prophecy in the music of that lonely stream wandering on to the Great Unknown. Too soon did she enter upon the fulfillment of that prophecy,—too long has that fulfillment been kept from me!

In the summer we went to school together, about half a mile away, to the old country district schoolhouse. I used to stop for her regularly in the morning on my way, and come back with her when school was out at night. Sometimes we played by the road-side, and then it would be sunset before we reached her home, and I would be left to go to my home alone. But it was not far—only a couple of hundred yards or so, and I always imagined she would be at my side to help me if anything should happen, which kept away fear. In the autumn she came again to see me—there being no school. Yet not so often, the weather was so rainy and blustering, and she was feeble in body. I was grown older, too, and they began to rally me about my little wife—some boorish loafers of the neighborhood. This made me ashamed to go and see her, and so we met less frequently. Yet her presence was ever dear to me, as the memory of it now. About that time it was she kissed me—only once—she never kissed me again, and the lie was told which conscience has ever treated so benignly.

Thus the first year—the outer circle of my recollection—passed on, becoming a treasure without price.

The next summer I was a great deal older. I began to play marbles with larger boys, and had a ball; and I did not care so much about being with Seraph—that was the little girl's name. Yet we were sometimes together as of old—played and walked together, and gave each other apples and keepsakes.

When winter came again, I went to school and she stayed at home, and I saw her so seldom that I became quite alienated, so much so that when one day it was announced to me that she had gone to stay a year with a maiden aunt living at a distance, I did not care much about it, though a few days afterwards I had a melancholy spell of an hour or two—that was all.

At school I made considerable proficiency, attaining to easy reading in a little time. The first impressions made upon me by reading, which I retain now, were of Poor Tray—world-renowned. That simple story entered deeply into my heart, the deeper, perhaps, because of a circumstance which I will relate. It happened during the summer which Seraph was absent.

Some three quarters of a mile from the school-house was a little artificial pond, belonging to one Abel Toom, a bleak old man who had died in his youth—if he ever lived—leaving a hide-bound skeleton, moving and existing, a social incumbrance—a most dismal-looking object, indeed; he was an incorrigibly selfish being too, not altogether free from the charge of villainy. This old man guarded his pond—because, forsooth, it had a few lean fishes in it—with the most jealous care, encouraging nests of snakes at different points along the bank thereof, and being present himself upon most occasions, uttering hideous imprecations whenever any encroachment seemed impending. But I had never heard of his having done bodily harm, though often hearing of the ludicrous figure he cut in view of trespassing youngsters.

One sultry afternoon in the latter part of summer, I was beset after school by a boy several years my senior, with the request to join a party that was going to vex old Abel, and if he should not be there, to go in a-swimming. I did not want to go on account of the company, and urged some reasons. These he met with so much derision, taking an oath that he would carry me down and duck me, and also including under his oath that he would tell the boys what a chicken-hearted fool I acted like, that, partly through fear, partly though spite, and a little through inclination, I acceded to his proposal. They were bad boys, and I knew it, but I went with them:—Poor Tray!

Arrived at the pond, no Abel in sight. We at once divested ourselves of clothing and went into the water. After amusing ourselves for a time, it was suggested to take a ride in a boat, which was moored near by where we were. The suggestion was enthusiastically acted upon, and we were soon in the deep waters, paddling away towards the middle of the pond, which was about a hundred yards across. We were in the midst of our enjoyment, one boy—the oldest—amusing the rest with a string of gratuitous jokes at old Abel's expense, when—bang! went a gun from the shore whence we had taken the boat. What was it for? The next moment we knew. Oh, flesh and bones! what a smart! Oh!—cruel, intolerable smart! "Salt!" cried one boy. "Salt! salt!" cried another. "Salt, and thunder! he'll kill us," chimed the third, and they all jumped out into the water like so many frogs, leaving me alone, and swam for the opposite shore. I yelled lustily to them to come back and help me out of danger, as I could not swim nor row. But they plashed away, swimming desperately, and paid not the least attention to me.—Poor Tray! I grabbed up the oars frantically, and attemped to use them; but between my awkwardness and confusion they both got out of my hands into the water. While striving to recover them, bang! went the gun again. I fortunately escaped with but few grains of the second charge, but fear took complete possession of me. I jumped up and down in the boat and screamed in the wildest manner. Nothing could be more certain than a lingering death on the spot, I thought. A stray breeze wandered over the pond, which proved quite refreshing to me—it was so cooling to my burning skin—until I became aware that it was wafting me directly towards the place where stood the awful old man, whom I had conjectured from the first to be, and now saw clearly was, old Abel himself. Utter despair set in, and I sank exhausted, and shrunk, lying flat in the bottom of the boat. In an incredibly short space of time the boat came within reach of a hook attached to a long pole in old Abel's hand, and the next instant the boat, with what there was left of me in it, was brought with a tremendous jerk upon the land. The bony hand grasped my arm. Death now was inevitable, and would be immediate —such was my vivid impression. But my dreadful apprehensions were directly dispelled by a great flood of surprise at his actions. "Ahasuerus Munn's boy, by G—d!" he growled, inspecting me. The discovery of my parentage seemed to astonish him a little, and abate his thirst for vengeance. He gently rubbed me all over with the palm of his hand, applying water now and then, until the intense smarting was considerably assuaged. Perceiving the effect of his remedial efforts, he led me around to my clothes —in the presence of which I almost cried, so long it seemed since I had put them off—and helping me on with them, he bade me go home quickly, and never be caught around his pond again—intimating more dreadful consequences in case I should be so caught.

I went home; and as I went, the analogy between

me and poor Tray arose distinctly upon my mind, and I felt almost like a brother to the little dog.

I made more progress in reading and spelling, doing my school-mistress great honor, if her tale to my parents can be credited. The autumn came, and slowly went. Winter school again commenced, and under a new tutor I was initiated into the study of Geography. Anticipatory as I have always been, I had hardly become accustomed to my new book before I made search, and found the map of Pennsylvania—my native State: and the very next place I looked for, after finding the shire-town of the county in which I lived, was that in which Seraph was staying. The impulse to look was altogether instinctive; but when I became clearly conscious of what I was about, a train of very moving recollections came upon me, diverting me wholly from my search. I wanted to see her very, very much. I lost all interest in my studies, and even in my sports, and went around that day feeling quite melancholy. It was gone, however, with the day; but not till after I had questioned my mother concerning the dear one's return.

The winter lengthened, lengthened, getting tedious

from its length, growing more and more tedious, until resignation took the place of despondency, and the hope for spring began to beam, and to point more confidently to the immediate future. Then the snow went off, beginning its aquatic journey one morning before light, and in two or three days it was all gone, carrying fences and barns with much live-stock from the bottom lands, and gouging many ravines of various depths—some quite formidable—in the bluffs. Three very exciting days, cloudy and misty—every sound, familiar and unattractive at other times, having strange loudness. After these days it was warm and pleasant. The grass began to grow; the birds to sing; the cattle went out upon the pastures. It was spring. Yet Seraph came not. The arrangements regarding her stay had been changed. She would not be at home until mid-summer.

As the spring came tenderly, genially on, I was taken sick. A long illness it was, and painful, wasting me to skin and bones. For a time it was thought I never would recover. But nature prevailed at last. Before the summer, I was well again. It was during this illness that I first realized a mother's love, a mother's kindness; gentle sisters' devotion, a father's solicitude. Though it was many years before I learned the relative character of those who surrounded and administered unto me during this illness, yet, as I first began to perceive it then, and as it seems to me necessary to introduce them to you at this point, I will attempt a sketch.

My mother was an excellent, old-fashioned woman —a kind of standard work on goodness and social propriety; faithfully attendant upon the sick and afflicted; always cordially the same to those with whom she associated. She was a thinking woman, too, and passably well-read—often speculating upon abstract subjects at the tea-table, to the edification of female neighbors or sojourners, to whom she was administering the rites of friendly entertainment or of hospitality. She had been blessed with a good education in early life, a sound culture, being indoctrinated thoroughly, and sometimes spoke in public on the theme of a judgment and a world to come. All in all, she was quite a prominent character in the community, and was pointed out to blooming daughters as an example worthy of their close imitation.

My father was an austere man, being socially

armed and equipped, impregnable always, and dealing out his personal cordiality homœopathically. Yet in a general way he was a friend indeed. Worldly goods had accumulated almost insensibly around him until he could call his own much more than he needed. In fact, he was wealthy, and being orthodoxically temperate, and unambitious of pecuniary distinction, he naturally felt the surplus a burden, and obedient to his impulse, he annually gave away, in one direction or another, hundreds of dollars. His specious mansion was always open, and often seemed like a public-house, except that those who partook, did so without money and without price. He had been a farmer from his youth up, and delighting more in muscular than in mental exercise, his development had been chiefly in the former capacity. Still he was a man of excellent sense and every-day judgment.

I had two sisters, one of them six, the other ten years older than I. They were happy girls—plump, and rosy with health, perfect fountains of good nature, and unquenchable enjoyment. Morning, noon or night they were ever ready with smiles and pleasant words to contribute happiness where it was due. In intellectual peculiarities they were more after my father's than my mother's mould, being bright and apt, with good sense in practical affairs.

We three were the only scions of the parent stock, and most harmoniously did we live together. Yet being so much older than I, they were not exactly companions for me, and I felt it never more than during my slow recovery that spring. Besides, the elder sister, Delia by name, had begun to look with tender glance upon a certain young man in the vicinity, not very tender, but accompanied with a kind of melancholy, and a mental absence which withdrew her from me to some degree. I longed for Seraph to come home. Though somewhat diverted by my associations at school, yet the desire deepened. At last she came. Bright, and cheerful as ever, she met me. She was grown much larger, yet looked the same in her sweet face,—was the same prattling creature. I stayed at home a week on purpose to visit her; and oh, the hours were happy and swift. The week was gone quite too soon. Thenceforward I was never alienated from her. I had become used to the excitement and novelty of attending school, and participating in the sports of my mates; I had ceased to be disturbed by the taunts of coarse wretches; and I took her to my heart again more intelligently, more sincerely. She became as a sister to me, devotedly loved.

Happy in a father's and a mother's love, happy in sisters' love, happy in the companionship of Seraph; at harmony with my schoolmates, flattered and caressed by my tutors, I advanced smoothly along, developing in all human respects rapidly. One after another my pet sports passed out of fashion with me. Playing marbles first, then the pleasant variety that I drew from a little dog which one of my uncles gave me. Afterwards my kite with its dreamy liftings-up of my earnest soul, my fishing tackle next—then my bow and arrows. One by one they engaged me, and were laid by, having lost their attractiveness, and I came pensively, seriously into that leafy passage of life, where, green to the centre, everything appears green, hopeful, brilliant, alluring.

About thirteen years old I was. My sister Delia, full of ripeness and love as it is in woman's nature to be at twenty-three years, had not resisted the twining advances of that certain young man, but had linked soft tendrils around his manly heart, drawing him closer, and they were married—as healthy, honest, and mutually enjoyable a couple as ever went out on moonlight nights, to sit in fragrant arbors and kiss each other's lips, thinking this world a paradise.

In the midst of high rejoicings, of congratulations, blessings and glowing hopes, they retired from amongst us, going to a neighboring town to set up a new home of their own.

This was an era in our family. A new entry was made in the family-Bible, on a new page, and an entire overhauling and shifting took place, ending in a new arrangement of all the old, familiar objects, making the whole house appear strange for some time. But everything settled down quietly after a while, and, old habits resuming sway, we became gradually accustomed to the loss, so that matters went on pretty much as before.

As I had grown older, my intercourse with Seraph had become slightly tinged with reserve. She had become perceptibly timid in her bearing towards me. Still we met often, met by ourselves. But she would not let me take her hand or put my arm around her waist as I used to. There was a feeling within me, too, that forbade it. An inclination and a drawing back I had, and they both grew stronger. We had begun to love each other—not as brother and sister. Yet it was a bud that never bloomed!

One Monday morning in the summer after the marriage of my sister, which I ought to have before stated happened in April, I was surprised, on entering the school-room, to find Seraph's desk vacant—the more so as the school had already been commenced some time. Her regularity in attendance had been remarkable; and I could not divest myself of the apprehension, that some evil had befallen her. I thought of it many times during the day, and made bold to inquire, immediately on my return home, if they knew where she was. "Sick," said my mother. "I have just come from there; she is very sick." The announcement was for the moment like a dagger in my heart. I went away to my little bed-room up-stairs and cried. You may wonder somewhat at the depth of my attachment at that early age. I have wondered at it myself sometimes. Yet when I recall the singular earnestness of my disposition; the thousand circumstances that favored our intercourse; the exclusiveness of my affections, particularly towards females; the truly lovable character of the child, and her attachment to me; my predisposition for things and persons amiable and mild, being never fond of boisterous sports;—when I recall these things, it does not seem strange. To be sure I had cronies among boys of my own age, and of similar cast, yet these attachments were brief—changing constantly. There was a social want—it had been always with me—which none but Seraph could meet. That want was taking another and deeper hold. Hence, my solicitude.

The next evening I inquired again with a trembling voice. My mother was very sober. "My son," she answered, "I am afraid our Seraph is going to die."

"Can I go and see her?" I asked, overpowered with anguish.

"She is delirious," replied my mother. "She would not know thee." Oh, how it wrung my heart to hear this! I could eat no supper. And when I went to bed I could not sleep, I could think of nothing but her. I would not go to sleep. It seemed a sin for me to sleep, and she lying in so much pain—so sick. When at last, long after midnight, I began to dream, it was of her; yet of her in health, leading me by the hand through an endless mead of flowers and shrubs, and lofty trees.

I did not go to school the next day, nor the next.—The third day she died. My mother was with her when she died. They would not let me go, though I entreated with tears. It was well perhaps, they did not. My memory of her now, is as of a sweet vision that beams awhile, passing back to heaven.

When my mother returned from composing the remains of the little sufferer, I asked her to tell me how she died and what she said. With much interruption from tears and sobs, she told me, that a few minutes before her death, she revived from the stupor into which she had fallen, and called her father and her mother to her side, and kissed them saying, "We will meet in heaven, dear father and mother; good bye." "Then she beckoned her sisters, one after another," continued my mother, "and they came, and she kissed them, begging them not to weep so, telling them she was happy, and would be a great deal happier soon. Her brother was kneeling by her. Oh, it was hard for him! Strong man as he is, he wept, and groaned, as though she were his last earthly friend. She told him to call me. I went to her. I bent over her, and smoothed her hair away from her forehead and kissed it. 'Thou art a good woman,' she said; 'I love thee. Good bye!' I was going away. I could not bear to see the little angel die. She clung to my hand, and asked me—'Is Ahasuerus here?' I told her no. 'Then tell him,' she said,—her voice was very faint; she was almost gone,—'tell him not to mourn for me. I am going to heaven, where I shall be always happy. I shall think of him. Give him my little Bible. Tell him to keep it. Don't let him mourn for me.' This was all I heard her say, my son. It is hard, I know," she continued, seeing me so overwhelmed with grief. "She was very dear to us all." The great Searcher of hearts, only knows the agony of that hour to me. I cried until I had no more tears to shed, walking about, at rest nowhere. It was cruel, indeed, and hard to bear. I went to my sister's room, and with her I talked over all I could remember of Seraph. It gave me great relief. Yet it was late in the night before I could be persuaded to go to my rest. When at last I did, my grief would not let me sleep. I felt as one in a strange place. I was! The world had changed to me. It would never be the same to me again.

Circumstances compelled it, and they buried her

the day following her death. I attended her funeral. But I did not look into the coffin. No one looked into it. When the ceremony of burial was over, and the throng had dispersed, I lingered, seating myself beneath a tree, a little apart from the grave, and feeling as though I could never leave the sacred spot. I sat a long time there, looking through my tears upon the grave so precious, recalling the thousand, thousand things that had a voice of her, that brought her beaming smile. Did her spirit linger, too, around that grave, soothing my sad heart with its new breath, and giving vigor to my memory? I had a grateful sense that it was so; and a sweet, tender melancholy, like that which sad, distant music gives, stole over me. I ceased to weep. My vision became clear, and I looked up through an opening in the trees, far up, deep into the soft, pure sky. There is her home, I thought. There she will hover, looking down upon me. There I shall go with her, when I die.

At last the cold night dews and the approaching darkness admonished me of the necessity of seeking my home; and with a slow, reluctant step I left the place. As I was going out, I met my father coming for me. He did not chide me; but took my hand in his tenderly, as was not his manner, and we walked home in silence beneath the gathering shadows of the silent night.

Grief may be very poignant, and deep, in early life; but it does not last. We are climbing the hill. The prospect is widening. Hope, too, is mounting; and the aerial view beams ever more brightly, becomes ever more vast and alluring. We overlook the graves of those who go aside, journeying no more with us,—they are lost in the swelling, gorgeous scene. We cannot stop, if we would, to hear the voice of the pine, or bedew the cypress. It is true, a great bereavement will make an era in opening life, will change the path from what it would have been. Still we must go onward, ever onward, on our way. This was to a great extent true of me. At first I went often to Seraph's grave, taking with me the little Bible—her last bequest. Every day I used to go. Then every other day. Finally but once a week. And when the winter snows came, their whiteness lay unsullied around that grave—no, there was one track. I saw it as I was passing once: a woman's track. I stopped to look at it; but the place appeared bleak and desolate; I did not enter. "When spring comes," said I to myself, promisingly, and passed on. So soon had it become a pious duty merely.

Spring came; but with it came other thoughts—new, and new feelings, new objects of interest. One afternoon in the latter part of April, as I was hoeing in the flower-garden, in front of the house, a middle-aged man, carrying a large portmanteau, came up to the gate, and asked if Ahasuerus was at home. Since Seraph's death, my sister Cynthia had persisted in calling me by my proper name, and I had got the hang of it pretty well. For the moment forgetting that Ahasuerus was likewise my father's name, I advanced, hoe in hand, very confidently, and told him yes, that was my name. "Well, you've met with a great loss of years," he responded, "that's a fact, since I saw you. I'd like to partake of your elixir, myself. By the by, boy, it's your father I want to see; Ahasuerus Munn, senior." Though mortified at my blunder, yet such was his manner—so full—overflowing with heartiness and the most sunny good-nature, that I suffered no self-depreciation; and I informed him, in a very civil way, that my father was at work in an adjoining field. "Indeed! Industrious as ever. Why, the man will be rich one of these days, I'm afraid," he said, coming through the gate, and looking around admiringly. The open front-door caught his eye. "Well, I suppose it's no difference. Cynthia, and Delia, and the good, strong-minded Catherine—mother of us all, I might say,—they're at home, not?"

"Delia is married, and gone away, this spring's a year," I replied, answering his question, and giving him the fact as something that would interest him, I thought, from his manner. And it seemed to, much. "Married!" he broke out in great astonishment. "Delia married? Boy, I'll have you beheaded for making false report. You really say, on the oath of an honest boy—which I confess you resemble—that Delia Munn, my little knee-high pet, is married, and gone off—this spring's a year. Well, now; that beats Croton oil. I had no idea time was passing *so* fast. And I never heard of it either. That's strange. Yet's a long while, I know. By the by, this puts me in the way of thinking there was a little squalling brat, nibbling silver tea-spoons in the cradle, and laughing at the looming spectacle of feet, to the ownership of which he did not see his title clear. A lusty brat he was—only son he was, too,—heir apparent. Are you he?"

I replied that I supposed I was.

"And has it come to this?" he mused, surveying

me from head to foot, and resting his hand upon my shoulder. "My boy, you and I must be better acquainted. Don't you remember me? Lord, no. That was a foolish question. Haven't you ever heard your father or mother—mother, most likely—mention the name of Joshua? That's"——

At this moment some one appeared at the front door. It was my mother. "Um!" she exclaimed—a favorite expression of surprise with her, and the nearest approach to a by-word I ever heard her utter—"Joshua!"

"Catherine, as I live! The never-to-be-forgotten Catherine, how do you do?" The next moment he had hold of her hand, and a cordial greeting ensued. "Grown a little old in the mean time; I hope not cold?" Her bearing did not seem to indicate it. "And Cynthia, too—dear child! How you bloom!" Cynthia held his other hand. "I loved you once, you chick, and used to kiss you. You're only a chick*en*, now, and I see no objection"——Smack! "Ay, it's over with. You needn't blush so. Take thought on my grey hairs. Indeed, how have you all done in the long interval? Well, I see. Delia is married, they say. By the everlasting hills, I was surprised. I could not have been more so if the Man in the Moon had accosted me." There was a pause in which all three seemed to be thinking seriously about something. "Thou art well, I see, friend Joshua," said my mother, returning to the subject. "Always well, Catherine," he responded, having the appearance also of returning; "haven't been sick an hour in the last five years."

"I'm glad to hear thee say so," said my mother. "We have to thank a beneficent Providence on that account, ourselves. But come in. Supper will be ready soon. Deacon, call thy father." Upon this they went in, and I went to discharge my behest.

With a little of the hypocritical, as I had begun to be mischievously inclined sometimes, I merely called my father to supper; and walking along with him into the house, enjoyed his surprise exceedingly. "After five years' interval, how do I find you?" inquired Joshua, rising. My father responded cordially, exhibiting more emotion than I had ever seen in him before. They directly fell into a very animated conversation, Joshua doing the principal part of the talking, expressing both his thoughts and recollections and my father's to a great extent. I listened until I began to lose interest in what they were saying; and then I gave way to the speculation which had infested my mind ever since he first addressed me, namely, as to who he was. He was an old acquaintance of the family: that was evident. He was a doctor,—so I had gathered from the conversation between him and my father. From Harrisburg, I had gathered from the same source. I wanted to know more about him. Singular old man! I loved him. I could not help it. They all loved him. I could see that plainly. I called Cynthia aside and she satisfied me. He was an old school-mate of my father's and mother's. They had been to school many a year together. In his youth, Joshua had studied medicine, and had followed his profession very successfully in C—— (our county-town) and vicinity. Before she could remember, he had gone to Harrisburg to live. He had been to our house once since: this she could remember. And she had seen him five years before, when she and father and mother were in Harrisburg. I could remember when they went. "He is a bachelor," concluded my sister, "and isn't he a nice man?"

"I like him," said I.

"So do I," she said. "He's the best man in the world."

Armed with these facts, I returned, and we all sat down to supper. The conversation shot off in various directions, without coming back to any given point, wandering very desultorily, touching upon one thing and another, at last hitting me. "I see that said baby—pride of a mother's heart—has grown monstrously," remarked Joshua, looking apparently awestricken at me. My mother assented modestly, and I blushed. "Let's see, he's fourteen, according to my reckoning, not?"

"The fifth of next month," answered my mother promptly.

"Fourteen. Long years to him, I have no doubt, longer than to the rest of us. Deacon, I observe you call him. Do you deserve the name, my boy? I know a very worthy deacon in Harrisburg. Deacon,"—I was blushing deeply, and they were all smiling—"you ought not to be ashamed of your name." The conversation was painful to me, and he knew it; so he changed it.

The supper, and afterwards the evening, passed off very pleasantly, and we retired to sleep, Joshua bearing his huge portmanteau with him—"Not for fear of robbery," he observed, "but for fear I shall want to rob it myself."

I was just about dropping into slumber, when a sound like vocal music from Joshua's room, which was adjoining mine, jerked me broad awake. Music was a thing comparatively unknown in our parts, particularly in our house, and it startled me. I listened. Joshua was evidently in great anxiety wrestling with the pitch. Presently he captured it and started off with an eminently successful pace as it regarded sound, rising majestically into the labyrinth. Directly his pitch was gone. He did not seem at first aware of it. When he was, he stopped. After a short skirmish on the spot, he went on again, finishing with another piece altogether, whose end was so much too low for his voice that the last three or four notes put me in mind of trying to duck a cat. I was amused. Though unversed in the science of music, I had some sort of an idea what it should be. I have by nature a good ear; and through the medium of a small Methodist congregation which met for worship in our town, and which I sometimes out of curiosity had mingled with, had gained a little incidental cultivation. I perceived that Joshua's effort was a laughable failure, but he did not. Far from it. He seemed to draw inspiration from his imaginary success, and glowingly tramped through one piece after another for a half an hour or more, whistling through the heights which his voice could not reach, and coming to an end only by reason of the interruption of a violent cough, which he could not surmount, nor disguise.

The next morning at breakfast, my father, in a rallying way, asked him how he slept. He took the point, and replied, with a slight dash of embarrassment at first, "Well, quite well. Better than the rest, maybe, eh? I declare I didn't think of your private sentiments last night. I *did* get warm—unusually so. But there is a power in those old masters, by their manes! Ahasuerus, if I had followed music as a profession, I believe I might have done something. All my voice needs is careful training. But that, you know, a man of my calling can't do very well. I understand the science perfectly. I wish I could jot down some of my conceptions, and had a voice to sing them, *I'd* show these squalling, caterwauling popular vocalists how the thing *should* be done. I never heard any music yet that sounded to me like music—except perhaps in dreams.—By the way, that brings up the dream I had last night. You must hear it. I dreamt that Mozart came to me, and sang so vehemently, and with such exalted inspiration, that the notes took material shapes and fell out of his mouth upon the ground. I picked them up, and they gave out, each according to its size, the most exquisite tones imaginable. I awoke trying to get the key note into my ear. Mozart had told me if I could get the key note in, he would repeat his song. Quite a dream wasn't it? However, I know your constitutional objections to the subject."

"By no means. Go on Joshua," my mother put in. "Sing, and talk about it all thou pleasest. We are commanded to bear with one another's infirmities," she concluded, smiling.

"Yes, yes, I know. But never mind, my tale is told. Let us dismiss the subject."

During the forenoon and a part of the afternoon, being engaged at my appointed task, I did not see Joshua. Towards night, as I was sitting on the gate-post, taking boy-fashioned repose from my labor,

Joshua hailed me from the front door, asking me if I wished to walk. Eagerly assenting, I joined him and my father, and we strolled off, away down across the old meadow towards an ancient forest, bounding its opposite edge. The sun was about two hours high, shining peacefully, and with a mellow light, upon the silent, majestic trees, all along the side we were approaching, filling the fresh foliage, as it were, with living light, and imparting a most delightful sense of repose to the soul.

As we walked leisurely on, looking around at different objects of attraction,—now each for himself, —now all together, looking in silence, except a brief remark or ejaculation now and then, Joshua had a train of thought suggested to him, apparently by the general scene. I remember the theme.

"Could we always see the world under such a light," thought he aloud, "I would be very much better contented in it. Could we always feel within ourselves such balmy influence shed abroad, see it and feel it, how much more bearable were human life! I have watched men considerably one time and another, and I have always found them at this hour, when the heavens were open and the earth responsive, in better mood, more susceptible to the appeals of distress, more open to the reception of sound thought, more suggestive of it. Is it not so?"

"Yes, I believe it is," replied my father, endeavoring to express in his countenance the philosophical depth which his words did not convey.

"I have found genius beginning its day of action at this hour, shadowing forth great things that were to live in the hearts of men for ever," continued Joshua in general. "The criminal, it is said, lays aside his bloody machinations, feeling the sweets of remembered purity at such an hour, beneath such a scene. Then—it is said—the breath of ripened beauty is balmiest, her words more of the tone of heaven. Hope is most quiet, memory most active, devotion nearest to its God. Indeed mankind is better. It is a blessed hour. Poets have sung about it, lovers have loved it, dying saints have thanked God for it; and I thank God for it, thank my stars for it. Ahasuerus!"

Ahasuerus, my father, had all the time looked very profound; starting up, he answered—

"What?"

"I'm thinking," said Joshua at the top of a long

breath, "that we've got to climb this fence." Sure enough, we were right upon the meadow fence—a nine-railed barrier. But we were soon over it, there being a little emulation in the act, and entered with a slower pace the grand old wood. Directly, Joshua remarked, "There's a tree that puts me in mind of a laughable thing that happened when I was a student, a great many years ago. Old Doctor Schaum,—you didn't know him, I guess."—My father *had* seen him once or twice.—"Indeed! You know his make then. He weighed three hundred and ten pounds avoirdupois, with his boots and cane,—plump that before dinner. I never could induce him to be weighed after dinner; for with all his grossness he had a delicacy about revealing the extent of his libations and sacrifices to the god, whose diadem is the waistband. He was very indolent in body; and he cherished his indolence with a sort of pride. This pride took for its object one significant fact of which he frequently boasted—namely, that he had never been forced by any earthly circumstance out of a *walk* since laying aside his short clothes; and he often in connection with this boast advanced the wish to be able to die with the consciousness, that the pace most consistent with human dignity had never been violated by him, since arriving at years of discretion. This eccentricity, so often exhibited, and with such seriousness, came to be, in the eyes of his friends and acquaintances, a fixed stratum in his character. It was when I was studying with him that the affair happened which I'm going to tell you about. It had been long brewing, but could not come to bead. At last a fellow-student—a splendid chap—since dead, poor fellow !—brought it about. Without communicating his design, he persuaded me to act a part. He said he wanted me to take a loaded rifle, and go to a certain point,—which he described exactly,—at a certain hour on a day mentioned, and post myself, watching cautiously. The day came. Oblivious of what was in the wind, I took the rifle, which was carefully loaded, and proceeded to the place. My post was at the corner of a large field, or square inclosed, in the suburbs of the town, not far from the doctor's house. On a diagonal line from where I stood, about fifty yards off, was a large tree, the only one in the field. On casting about to discover the object of my being there, I saw an animal, which from a mere glance, I took to be an ox, grazing quietly near the corner, first to the left from where I was. I had been standing there nearly an hour, and was beginning to get impatient, when the creaking of a large gate away over nearly to the opposite corner, attracted my attention. Looking sharply in that direction, I discovered that it was the old doctor entering the inclosure. He was coming from the direction of his house, and was crossing the field, evidently to save distance, as in his pedestrian tours he was always up to. Solemnly and steadily, he came on straight towards me. Busied with concocting an excuse, which I knew I should have to furnish him for being there, I did not pay further attention to him, until I heard a low, ominous bellowing. Looking up, I saw the supposed ox, pawing the ground, and shaking his head fiercely at the doctor, who, becoming suddenly aware of his situation,—being as he was, though considerably past the middle of the field, yet some distance from the corner,—quickened his pace perceptibly. I saw through the plot at a glance. Ha! ha! Go it guns! Now, old man—now for a run. Ay, my old doctor;—but no, he wouldn't run; no earthly circumstance should force him out of the cherished pace. Yet when he saw the rampant animal start, and with tremendous bounds, annihilate the distance between them, I believe he would have run, had he not at about the same moment seen me, and also discerned, by my contortions, the state of my mind. He was about sixty yards from the tree, which was his nearest point of safety, if it could be deemed anything more than a safety-*valve* in his case.

On came the fierce animal, shortening the protecting span of distance with amazing rapidity; and on came the glowing doctor, now in that doubtful province, between a walk and a run. But he would not run,—no sir; no earthly circumstance should bring him to that. He expressed this unequivocally. I could see it in the toes and heels of his boots, in the sweep of his cane, in the wrinkles of his pantaloons, in the set of his hat. "But you'll have to run," said I aloud, with a dash of apprehension. My apprehension deepened. I began to fear he would sacrifice his life to the eccentric notion. Accordingly I drew my rifle to my eye. He was near the tree.—The dreadful bull—a bull, and no mistake, was within three bounds of him. There was a moment, I did not look at the doctor. When 1 did, he was behind the tree, the bull goring the roots on the opposite side. It was not over yet, I perceived. After expending a part of his fury on the tree, the angry animal attempted to outflank his victim. This was trying to the doctor; yet he held his own nimbly and well, for so huge a bulk. But the bull's rage held on, and the doctor's strength began to give out. He was failing rapidly. The bull's horns once or twice caught in the skirt of his coat. There was but one chance for him; to divert the enemy a little, and *run* for the fence. Life was sweet—plum-puddings, and canvas-backs were sweeter. Weighty considerations. Indeed, there was no other alternative but death or life; bull-pudding or plum. Wise old physician, approved of the faculty, well-esteemed! He snatched his red-silk handkerchief from his pocket, whipped it around his cane, and shaking it in the face of the foaming beast, threw it as far as he could. The bull pursued it, *and the doctor ran* to the best of his ability. Reaching the fence, he rolled over bodily, falling upon the ground. "Oh, hold me!" screamed a voice in my ear, and a hand grasped my arm, convulsively. It was my fellow-student, completely beside himself with mirth. Fearing the doctor's vengeance, we vanished speedily. What became of the old man's wrath I don't know. He never manifested it at all. Neither did he thereafter ever indulge, before us two at least, in his time-honored boast." While Joshua was relating, this we had gone some distance into the forest. "I never was better pleased than with this," observed Joshua, referring to the scene. "These grand, old trees make me think of ages past away. Ahasuerus, Indians have looked upon these trees—Indians that had never heard of white men. Think of that. Don't it take you back?"

"Yes, it *does*," responded my father with dry emphasis.

"I love to wander," continued Joshua," in a good old wood. It makes me calm. There is a spirit in it:—mild, ancient spirit which I love. I co"—

"Hark!" interrupted my father with an expression of surprise and anxiety upon his face.

"Father!" It was the piercing cry of despair. It came from the direction of old Abel's pond, from which we were not far off. We ran. As we were running we heard the cry repeated fainter than before. "Help! help!" in a gruff yet agonized voice, echoed through the forest. We quickened our pace. In a few moments we were out of the wood in sight of the pond hard by. Joshua and my father were several yards ahead of me, and I, not feeling that I could be of any use, halted to look. In the middle of the pond was a boat upset, and a short distance from the shore was a greyheaded man swimming desperately, yet making but little progress, towards the boat. By the time Joshua and my father had reached the shore, the former had divested himself of his upper clothing, and without halting he leapt like a deer far out into the water, and swam for the boat. Just before he came to it, the head of a boy arose swayingly above the surface near him. With a skillful movement Joshua fastened his hand in the boy's hair, and wheeling, made for the shore. My father having in the mean time secured a rail from a neighboring fence, waded out, and with his assistance Joshua brought the insensible body upon the land. I was standing by when they brought it out, and recognized the features at once. It was old Abel's son—only child. He had once been a crony of mine. Samuel was his name. He was the best arithmetic scholar in the school. While I was running this over in an excited manner, standing around in the way, Joshua and my father were trying to bring him to life. Old Abel, having swam the whole length of the pond, came to their assistance; and after half an hour or so, they succeeded in restoring animation to the boy. Upon which old Abel took him in his arms tenderly, and bore him away towards his home, and we retraced our steps. As we were walking through the wood on our way home, Joshua remarked. "I wish I hadn't put a hand into that affair."

"Why?" said I, seeing my father paid no attention to the remark.

"Oh, I know the boy," he replied.

I remembered Sam had been for a few months past in Harrisburg, employed there as clerk in a dry goods store. I was about asking further explanation, when he resumed. "Deacon, I know you take it strange. But I don't like to see such boys grow up. He's of bad stock. And he's coming into possession of his legacy of meanness. That woman bequeathed it to him, cursed him with it. He should have drowned, ay, he should have drowned for all me, if I had known who it was before I went into the water. I would have left him on the shore there to die after we had him out but for a certain weakness I have—

force of habit. He should die, die young. The world don't need him. It didn't need—Oh, bitterness! Gall! gall!" His voice was clogged with emotion, and crossing his arms behind him he looked sorrowfully upon the ground.

"Thee should be charitable," calmly enjoined my father.

Between surprise and conjecture I was considerably excited, and I listened eagerly for Joshua's reply. But he made none. Neither did my father make any more remarks. They were both silent the rest of the way; and during the evening Joshua was sober, saying but little, and that reluctantly. What could it be that so disturbed him? It was long before I knew anything about it; and when I did, I only wondered he had not been more bitter—more cast down.

In the morning Joshua was himself again, only showing that he remembered the last night's adventure by avoiding allusion to it. Throughout the day, except at meals, I did not see him. During the evening he talked of music, discoursing two or three hours, elaborating a system which he intended to present to the world some day or other, he said. He was very tedious, I remember. If I had not surmised it before, I saw then plainly that with all his good qualities, and clearness of understanding, one thing was gone from him, if it ever made a part of him, namely, a power to perceive that the sphere of music was a forbidden realm to him; and that through fancying—yea, believing—it was not, he was making himself a laughing-stock, and oftentimes an incubus, where he might be winning love and commanding respect.

The baneful star reigned that night, until some time after he went to his room, and he again courted the "power of those old masters," getting a fit of coughing, and going to sleep, finally.

This monomania was the only unpleasant thing about him. I loved him more and more, the longer he stayed. He grew quite familiar with me, talking to me of subjects almost too abstruse for my untutored understanding, yet talking in so plain a way, bringing the thing out always so clearly, and was always so pleasant and patient with my foolish, at-random suggestions, unfledged imaginings, and disjointed analogies, that I loved him when most mortified, and could have sat, it seemed to me, for ever in conversation with him—except when music was his theme.

I would like to relate some more of the many things which I remember of him in connection with this visit, but I must hurry on to matters that will interest you more than these.

He stayed with us about three weeks. The hour of his departure was a sad one to me—sad to us all. It was a quiet, sunny morning, early. We stood at the gate, Joshua outside, his portmanteau slung upon his arm. Everything was so quiet. A dreamy sense, a reverie, rested upon us all—seemed to rest upon every living thing around us. We stood there, loth to say "good-by!" We were getting quite sorrowful. Something must be said, and Joshua said it beamingly, breaking the charm. "My very dear friends, I don't like such antitheses. This isn't the way you looked when I came here. You must bear in mind that me ye have not always, neither can. I am a bird of passage—of the species of vulture it is true. I am, too, superannuated. It is said, 'Time and tide wait for no man.' I do not ask them to tarry; but take Time by the forelock and lead him on his way and I laugh at the slothful tide. What's the use. This going back foremost into the Kingdom, I hold to be a shameful reversing of manly energies. When I go, I goeth, my friends; when I come, it is the same. No wind is more free, never was. When I love, I love. You know that, my good Catherine, you know that, Ahasuerus. And when I hate, I hate. You know that, too. I love you all. God knows my heart, I do. Catherine, good-by!"—He took her hand.—"You were kind to me once. May you shine the brighter in Heaven for it! Brave Ahasuerus, you are growing grey in the battle. Time is outflanking you. But be stout to the end. Good-by! That was an honest tear, Ahasuerus. Do you remember when you saw me weep? There was a desert around me then. It drank all the tears of my life,—a bitter yielding up, a greedy draught! Do not think me heartless. Cynthia, sweet girl, may you be blest. You deserve it. Love him,—I am serious now,—love him, but not with all your heart. Good-by! Deacon," he concluded, turning to me, "you're too young for such a strain. Be a good boy. Think sometimes of her who lies in that grove yonder. It will not hurt you any. I must hurry. Well, come and see me. I think now my business is so arranged that I can visit you oftener. I must. You will hear from me before long. Write." It was the last word, spoken as he hurried away.

My heart was heavy all that day. There was a

dismalness about the house, about the barn, in the field, the old forest;—upon everything in fact, associated with Joshua, rested an invisible shadow, which I felt. Nobody said anything at dinner, nor at supper, nor in the evening. Everything was quiet, very quiet. Towards bed-time, as I sat musing, generally impressed with Joshua in the various phases presented by my memory, my mind centered all at once upon some expressions in his valedictory of the morning. "Do you remember when you saw me weep? There was a desert around me then?" And what he said to my mother. "You were kind to me once." They were mysterious expressions to me. Yet my father and mother understood them. They seemed to shed tears more at them than at his going away. His remarks after saving the drowning boy, too:—they all referred to some passage of his life-history that had a deep and mournful interest. So much I conjectured; but could go no further. I wanted to know more. My parents could tell me. I would ask them.

"Father," said I, "what did Joshua mean this morning when he talked about thy knowing when he wept?"

My father made no reply; but in a minute or two

my mother said, looking solemnly at me. "My son, thy father must not tel. thee. Cynthia does not know, and thou must not." I knew it would be vain to push the matter, so I dropped it, reverting to his remarks again. There was something he had said which I could not at first recall. I could remember that it touched me deeply when spoken. But the expression. I strove to recall it for some time in vain. "Think of her who lies in that grove yonder!" That was it. My parents had told him of my bereavement, and his good heart had felt for me; and from that remark I saw that he had thought of me and her together, perhaps—it was but a dim conjecture then, which hardly took the form of thought—not wholly separate from his own youthful experience.

When I went to my room, which I did early, everybody and everything appeared so gloomy—I sought out the little casket in my trunk which contained the dear gift—the pocket-Bible that had once been Seraph's. I opened the precious volume, and read for the thousandth time the fondly remembered name. It had been written with a pencil, and was almost erased; still I could trace the lines in all their delicate windings; and, as was my custom, I traced them then; and they became, as they had always, a mirror held to the past—the sunny past. Peculiarly distinct were the oft-recalled impressions that night. With peculiar force they touched me. A sweet reverie, almost like a dream, came upon me; and for a long time I sat, or rather knelt there, before my trunk, holding the little volume, and looked into the magic mirror. I wandered—stopping here and there—back into the far perspective, even to the rivulet in the old meadow, and heard again its prophesy. But there was now something happy in the memory of its voice,—I had felt it before:—perhaps it was not the rivulet's voice alone:—it was something of Immortality. My soul caught the strain. Vibrating, it kindled my imagination, and a vision new and strange opened upon me. It was a vision of the future—of the distant future. It was very enrapturing, but brief, coming and fading like a blinding flash. Yet it turned the current of my thoughts. I closed the little book and put it away, and went to bed, wishing for that hour to come which would bring me to Seraph, and her to me, to be happy for ever, both of us.

The next day was the Sabbath. I attended at the

old place of worship with my parents. It was an unassuming, antiquated building, in its dotage, yet out of deference—I know no other reason—occupied still. It stood at a four-corners, nearly a mile from the village, and something over half that distance from our house. A peaceful location it was, like the congregation of quiet-loving spirits that had for more than half a century met there from time to time to do homage to their God. A pleasant grove surrounded the building, as if protecting it. In the grove were some pines — stalwart, ever holding legendary converse with the winds. The grave-yard was there in that grove, occupying the corner opposite the sanctified structure. How natural, how beautiful the sentiment of our fathers, that the dead must sleep where the living meet to worship!

After worship I went into the grave-yard. As I stood by the mound so hallowed, I felt to reproach myself quite bitterly that I had not been there oftener of late. Only the fourth time since spring had opened, and it was almost June. Yet the place had an enchantment about it. I felt it when I was there. Why did I not come oftener? I had not forgotten Seraph—oh, my heart! no. New objects had come to divert me. Upon the great Stream of Time I was being borne away. Yet it was not altogether these. I knew it then. There was a voice whispering to my secret soul—never more distinctly than on that serene Sabbath afternoon, while I stood looking upon the silent grave—that she, dear Seraph, was with me always, living, watching, communing with me. Her body was of earth—dust, her spirit a sentient being—of heaven. I lingered an hour or so, and then walked away homeward lightsomely. There was a change within me. I perceived it, yet did not remark it. I should no more look back, as for the last few months I had. Forward I saw—dimly, a glimpse—I saw a life opening before me. A life of realities, pleasant they seemed to me then, gorgeous realities. Then a going down into the Valley of Shadows, and a glorious uprising for evermore! I saw, and was happy. Who showed it me? Who taught my soul to believe it? I was what the world terms visionary then, though I had scarcely learned to think. I am so now, having learned. These things were not the offspring of my unaided mind. Seraph. She lives.

In a few days the general gloom which Joshua's

departure had brought down, passed off, and I resumed the routine of duties, manual and other, with cheerfulness and abundant hope. The summer went by genially, bringing, among its other natural productions, a long letter from Harrisburg, signed with a prodigious flourish, and a stray quirk or two, by way of ornament—"Joshua Noyles." It was a very amusing and interesting letter to all of us; and was read and re-read until, through fear of its total destruction, my mother locked it up in the bureau drawer, and we, that is Cynthia and I, gradually forgot it.

The autumn came, at once gay and mournful, as death should be. It was late in that season. Winter was showing itself on the mountains, impatient to begin its work in the silent valleys. It was a gloomy day. There were thick clouds in place of the sky, and it was cold. I had been husking corn in the field all day. As I came in from my work I was met at the door by Cynthia, who was so flushed and smiling that I knew she had something to tell me. "Who do you think has got home?" she asked, betraying by her form of expression what she evidently wished to conceal. I guessed right the first time, greatly to her surprise. "Fanny Cline," said I; "and I want to see her." I wanted to see her because she was Seraph's sister. She had been next in the series older than Seraph, and was now the youngest of the family. In times past I had been acquainted with her, yet never familiarly. She was about a year older than I, and while Seraph lived she had seemed so much older, that I hardly ever thought of her, except as an older sister, like Cynthia. The youngest now. There were two other sisters, considerably older, both married; and a bachelor brother, the eldest of the children; the father and mother, exemplary Friends and citizens, middle-aged, grey, weather-beaten, hardy people, and withal intelligent: such was the family of Clines.

Fanny, since Seraph's death, had been absent, staying with the maiden aunt, and was just returned, much increased in stature, and in beauty, too. So Cynthia said, as we walked in together. I found it true. I had used to think she was handsome, her cheeks were so red, and her lips; her eyes so sparkling; her long, silken hair, which hung and waved in such luxuriant ringlets; and more than all, the imperturbable cheerfulness of her disposition. Now she appeared beautiful, decidedly so. She still wore her hair loose. It was very luxuriant, of a dark auburn. Her eyes were dark and somewhat large, at once tender and sparkling as of yore—yet more tender. Her mouth was most exquisitely chiselled, and around it reposed, looking sweetest in repose, a peculiar expression which gave an exhaustless charm to her countenance. So I found her sitting in Cynthia's room, glowing with health—indeed the picture of it, it appeared to me. Perhaps it was not all that which made her so ruddy. I was glad to see her, because she was Seraph's sister; and in the excess of my friendship I kissed her. She was going to resist me; but I think she divined my sentiment, and received the offering approvingly. After the first ebullition, I was very calm, much calmer than she was. We talked together of the changes that had taken place since her going away, gravely, like older people. Then we talked of the more distant past; and spoke with subdued voices of the dear one. She wept, but I did not. She was very sad, and I strove to comfort her in the same manner as I had been comforted. I spun my efforts to considerable length, finding it very pleasant to talk to her,—so pleasant that I departed from the main object several times, becoming quite personal, toying with her soft hair—we were on a settee, side by side—and wadding up her handkerchief, much to her inconvenience. Finally she became cheerful, and we familiarly talked and laughed, mainly about the old clothes I had on, which began to embarrass me a little. Before that theme was entirely exhausted, the evening was up. I escorted Fanny home, feeling more and more foolish because of my apparel, and when I parted from her, before saying "good night," I had to offer a serious apology for my exterior.

The next day, at my work, I had a new theme of reflection. Yet I did not think so much as I felt on the subject. So beautiful she was. I believe every dozenth pulsation of my heart all that day, brought her image in some phase or other before me. Physical deformities of mine—and I was astonished as well as pained to find so many—became disagreeably prominent. It was a very long day, too: I seemed to have lived a week in it. Yet I was not in love, only beginning to be; quite earnestly, however, it must be confessed.

Fanny, Fanny, Fanny. I wrote it in the snow. I

wrote it on my slate. I wrote it very elaborately on an enamelled card, with ornamental touches in red ink—wrote the name in full, Fanny Cline. I showed the card to her when she next came to visit Cynthia, which was about a week after the interview described. It was about all I could do, I was so painfully embarrassed in her presence. The sentiment had grown upon me amazingly during that week. She praised the chirography exhibited on the card, and with a very sweet smile, told me that if I would do my own name in the same manner upon another card, she would keep it as a gift.

The two interviews, that is, the first and this, differed principally in character in her doing the most of the talking, and my becoming an enchanted listener. I could do nothing but smile. I felt very loose and buoyant; and when I attempted to steady myself into something like a dignified mien—which I experienced a growing necessity of—it seemed as though I had no foundation, and it was like steadying, or trying to, a very rampant balloon. I smiled on still, not saying anything that I could bear to recall; and when she went away, I labored under the general impression that I had acted a very silly part. Something must be done, I thought, or I should be for ever disgraced in her eyes. She would come again the next Sabbath evening, so she had told Cynthia. A petition was sent up, and to my surprise met with immediate attention, namely, to fit me out with a new suit of clothes, ostensibly for the purpose of appearing respectably at church—my then existing Sunday suit, it was urged, being inadequate to that end. Within four days I was fitted to my satisfaction. So much done. The card was written on next, very successfully. I was prepared. The Sabbath came—the evening. And Fanny came. When I thought she and Cynthia had been together a proper length of time, I went to her room, "dressed to death," and ushered myself into their presence. For a few minutes I succeeded in passing myself for a civil young gentleman in his teens, but the very first time Fanny looked into my face with that bewitching smile of hers, I relapsed helplessly into the old state, imbecile as ever. I brought forth the card, but her praises only sank me deeper. I reverted to my new suit. It did no good.—It was absolutely nothing, and worse, for I felt unworthy of the clothes. After a few minutes there was a reaction, and I felt better—only better. I knew I ought not to stay there and immolate my dignity in that manner. But I could not get away. Besides the allurement to remain, I knew that if I should attempt to break loose, all that had gone before would be swallowed up in the enormous awkwardness with which I should accomplish it. It was of no use. I was in the vortex, and as effectually lost as any poor seafaring wretch in the great maelstrom. I became patient and felt better still—quite refreshed, as one feels after a storm in hot weather. I actually made two or three remarks just before starting home with her, that I felt in some degree proud of.

When we parted that night, I dared to press her hand; warm and velvety it was, only these; there was no response. It was a desperate act of mine, and as I walked homeward, it occurred to me that possibly the rash venture had given her offence. The suspicion was anguishing, and I could not repel it. The only alleviation I had was the thought that the act was past recall, and I could only show by future conduct how much I reprobated it.

The next day, Monday, I commenced going to school. I was getting to be quite a large boy—a young man, I thought—so I went this winter to the village-school, a select affair, where everything was very prim, and advanced, things and scholars bearing the stamp of the tutor, a sickly young elder, who, being unable to perform his sacerdotal duties, had taken to teaching. I disliked him at first. His preciseness and dryness of manner sifted upon me suffocatingly, and I went home the first night regretting deeply that I had committed myself so much as to commence.

But I did not dislike him so much the second day. The third not so much. And when it came Saturday night, I found myself looking forward to Monday again, with some pleasure.

Sabbath evening, Fanny was at our house as usual. I had something to talk about that time, and as long as the fund lasted, I passed. But that was not long, and the first thing that visited me when I began to feel barren, was the remembrance of my foolish act in the dark, a week before. It crushed me for the instant quite flat, but I was directly comforted with the reflection that her conduct did not show that she remembered it, and—strange vicissitude of feeling!—a desire to do it over again sprang up. I had the escorting of her as usual. But it was very cold, and she kept her hands in her muff. Could I put mine in there too? Then I had a suspicion that it was not the dangerous weather either that made her so jealous of those pretty hands, though they were tender. But I was attending a select school, in the village. There were other girls. Handsome ones. I did not feel, therefore, so dependent as formerly. In fact, this time I was myself offended—a little. What changes! —apparent.

Notwithstanding, I thought of Fanny frequently that week, more towards the latter part, as the novelty of my new place was wearing away.

Sunday night again I saw her. The same sorry, unsatisfactory figure again I cut, or rather mangled. I never should mend it, so it seemed. That night, for the first time, I became sensible of a melancholy, on account of my dismal relation to the adored Fanny—adored now. I was in love in earnest, though not yet quite fifteen. To be sure I have had impulses of passion since, to which that was but a small lambent flame; but then it was as serious as it has ever been.

Sweet Fanny, I love thee. It was a secret thought,

first-sighed in secret with a gush of rapture. Then I ventured it upon my slate, written half of it at a time, and rubbed out instantly. Then out in full, to be looked at. Directly it was down on a piece of paper. The paper was torn up and chewed. Then it was very carefully written on fine paper in red ink —symbolic—and some other words were added including my given name. Saturday afternoon it was done. Sunday evening, in great agitation, I secretly slipped it into Fanny's muff as it lay on Cynthia's table. That night Cynthia went home with her. Why? I had not been private enough. Ay, I was caught! But I couldn't help it. And, in truth, I did not care. I'd not be ashamed of my feelings. Cynthia might laugh; but it wouldn't make Fanny less sweet. Alas! it might lessen me in her eyes. The thought was bitter, like nettles, and stung like them too. But I was launched. Things must take their course. This was my conclusion, and I went to bed upon it.

The week was long and fruitful of impracticable plans—I could not let things take their course—founded upon conditional circumstances. Plans as to my getting out of the scrape, or getting further into it, or getting along with it. I was, or fancied I was, indifferent as to which. I call them impracticable; for when Saturday night came, not one remained, and I ingenuously opened my eyes on the Sabbath to receive my renewed anticipation of the evening in as blank, unfortified a state as ever.

It grew dark very slowly that evening. The twilight clung like a stain. The stars came out reluctantly. The clock was unaccountably lazy, yet kept pace with the time. The phenomena almost made me feel superstitious. The time went slower and slower, and by seven o'clock it seemed to have stopped altogether. I could hold on no longer.

"Why"—I checked myself, fearing to betray irritation, and passing my hand over my face the more to mask my feelings, added, "How is Fanny to-day? Hast thou seen her?" to Cynthia.

"Yes, I saw her this afternoon," she replied, without looking directly at me. "She is well, very well."

I thought—indeed I was quite sure—I saw a nest of suppressed wrinkles struggling around her eyes and mouth, and the next instant I was submerged as it were with a tepid wave. All along through the day, and up to that moment, I had avoided thinking directly of the last Sunday evening's circumstance. Now I could not help it. And worse, I could think of nothing else. Oh, the night! For a youngster not much acquainted with real troubles—yet somewhat, too—I was very miserable. I had wounded the bird I would tenderly have caught, and she had flown. Until after midnight I lay wide awake in trial, striving to buckle on the panoply of indifference. I had at first some imaginary success. But there were two or three things that held out—among which my dignity. Chafed with the consciousness that a great fool had existed for the past month under my name, it would not yield, and in a state of total discomfiture I fell asleep.

During the week that followed, I increased my endeavors, not only to induce indifference towards what I had done, but towards the prime cause. I addressed myself to study with assiduity; and, as opportunity occurred, sought to enlarge my acquaintance among the young ladies of the school. In this latter I succeeded amazingly. I had had no idea I was so popular. I suppose there was something about me very pleasing to the other sex. At any rate there seemed to be from the reception I met with at once. All smiles and laughter they were, sacrificing themselves entirely to please me. It was agreeable, that's a fact, and diverted me—so far answering the purpose for which I had sought their society. With the social enjoyment thus afforded, and the new interest which my studies gave, I passed along very smoothly, getting through the next Sabbath evening with only a few sage reflections, in which there was some satisfaction; for the fact of Fanny's not being at our house confirmed me entirely in my supposition, which caused me to view the whole affair in the aspect of a necessary evil. I was quite philosophical for a youth—the more so, perhaps, for having just read a long letter from Joshua, which had, strangely enough, a good deal in it bearing pretty directly upon the question. Yet all the while I had a sense like being on thin ice over fathomless depths.

But the ice grew thicker, and time went steadily on. For several weeks, perhaps two months, I did not see Fanny, except at divine worship on the Sabbath, and that was the same as not seeing her at all. Accidentally—I had no reason to think otherwise then

—one evening as I returned from school, I met her between our house and hers. She was humming a scrap of music in a very lively mood, and said "good evening" to me with great cheerfulness of manner, but went straight by me, though I halted, for I had it in my heart to say something more. As I stood looking at her receding form, which seemed to float rather than walk, the depths throbbed—but the ice did not break.

It was getting to be spring. Harrow-shaped flocks of wild-geese, and vast flocks of pigeons were flying to the northward. The snow had mostly disappeared, clinging in a dull icy form only in obscure hollows, and here and there along the northern side of stone fences. Black-birds were making vocal the swamps and lowlands, and early flowers were springing up in the woods. The select school was closed, and I was at home working on the farm. It was a warm, serene day—cloudless, and full of hope. I was in the field pretending to labor, yet preferring rest, which I was indulging in at the time of which I speak. I was sitting on the fence, basking in the sunshine, and musing upon the events of the past winter. I was sad. Much as I had disliked my teacher at first, I had come to love him. He had been always kind to me, and now I was thinking of his kindness, of his misfortunes, and of the likelihood of my never seeing him again, as his health was very poor, and everybody said he would die soon. I was thinking of the hour of parting; how he ranged us in a semicircle, and shook hands with each, saying "good by!" and how the tears ran down his pale, hollow cheeks, as he went on in the painful ceremony, and how each one, when his or her turn was past, went away weeping. From these sorrowful recollections I was aroused by the sound of voices. I looked up, and saw Cynthia and Fanny approaching. They were coming leisurely across the field, right towards me. I thought they did not see me, and being afraid of becoming privy to their artless remarks, I leapt briskly off the fence and hawked sonorously. It was gratuitous.

"Lazy boy!" cried Cynthia playfully, "sitting on the fence all day. I'll tell father."

"How do ye do, ladies?" said I with a low bow.

"What?" inquired Cynthia, catching her breath in the midst of a laugh. I repeated the performance, which, from my confusion, proved a bad imitation.

"We are all well, except the family," she responded. Then they both laughed, Fanny blushing and looking down. I could see no point to the remark, yet I laughed as though I did, and so they came up to me, Fanny leaning on Cynthia's arm, looking so fresh and beautiful! It was going—the ice. I cast a stern glance at her as an anchor. I felt justified in so doing. Why should she tempt me?—the witch. For a moment—the smallest fraction of an ordinary moment—her eyes met mine. My soul! it was too late. The fountains of the great deep were broken up.

"Well, brother, how dost thou like work?" asked my sister soberly. I was smiling on Fanny—all smile it seemed to me—and answered. "Very well."

"Thou findest it rather hard I reckon," remarked Fanny, her voice musically sweet.

"Oh!" I commenced, as though in harmony with some imaginary music, then dropping to the key of practical life I ended, "rather hard." But I was not thinking of what she was. Daily labor was forgotten. I was very much confused.

To my temporary relief, my sister at this point discovered some beauty or oddity in my jacket buttons, and entered into an examination of them—tem porary; for in so doing she pulled Fanny close to me. The emanating glow of her healthful presence—I felt it flooding me with rapture. Cynthia induced her to touch with her finger one of the buttons she was examining. As she withdrew her hand, mine by strange coincidence was rising, and they met softly palm to palm,—but an instant; both withdrew as though each had touched a serpent.

"Cynthia, let us go back," said Fanny, looking towards the house and away from me.

"Well, as thou mindest," responded my sister cheerfully, and wheeling gracefully, they went away arm in arm as they had come—yet soberly.

"Oh, my angel!" I whispered fervently, my burning eyes resting upon the adored form. "Oh, misery!" loaded the next breath. "She does not love me. She will not love. What shall I do?" I was overwhelmed with melancholy. All that I had done to fortify myself—all my fancied security, gone as chaff. "Dear, dear Fanny. Cruel Fanny. She might love me. There is nothing hateful about me, I know. Other girls, prouder than she, are glad of my attentions. She shuns me as if I were wild and filthy, or wicked, and would do her harm."

There was no alleviation, except a little in uttering my woes. It was morning when the foregoing transaction came to pass. At noon I could eat nothing. "Thou art sick, my son," remarked my mother, feeling my pulse. I was.

"Let him work. That will cure him," said my father.

"Oh, no, father; he isn't well. Don't thee see? he is pale," expostulated Cynthia.

"I know what'll cure him," said my father, regardless. So did I.

That afternoon I did not work in the field. I went to my bed-room, and in the midst of sighs, groans, and some hot tears, gave birth to a few short, irregular stanzas upon the subject of love. Short and irregular as they were, they expressed volumes for me. I felt greatly relieved, so much so, that about four o'clock I went down and ate a hearty meal.

Still, a dim, and dimming shadow of melancholy remained—for days, weeks. It did not go away at all for the present.

Fanny did not come to our house except when I was at work in the field. She never was there when I was there. Why? Why? I frequently asked myself. At last, in a bold mood, I asked Cynthia. She did not answer me, and she blushed a little, I thought. I did not repeat. Thus matters went on. The spring passed, and the summer, nearly. It was late in that season, that a pic-nic was concocted. The fact was duly and formally made known to me by way of a note, requesting my attendance—with lady. With lady. Who should that lady be? Fanny would not go with me; and I would go with no one else. I guessed there would be no lady. Yet I must have a lady or stay at home. Some one might offer to take Fanny. Yes. But could I stand that? No. I would make an effort to get her. I penned a brief, formal invitation, and through the medium of Cynthia, had it conveyed to her. I was so much surprised when Cynthia handed me, on her return, a billet, that I blushed exceedingly—partly because I thought it was my own sent back. With pleasure my invitation was accepted. But it was merely a form. She might have written the same to anybody. So I thought; but, like a sensible youth, I quarrelled not with the thought, because it would come to nothing but bitterness. She had accepted my company. That should suffice.

The day appointed for the pic-nic came, and in good country style Fanny and I joined the party, and all went gleesomely away to a grove upon the bank of a large stream, three or four miles distant from my father's. The day passed in the happiest manner, and it was pretty far in the evening when we separated to go to our homes. During the whole of the joyous time, Fanny was the gayest of the gay; but when the company separated, and we were alone together, going homeward, she was silent. I made some casual remarks, to which she answered briefly, but her voice was mild—had a touch of pathos in it which thrilled me. Oh, how I loved those sweet accents! but could not utter my love.

It was dark when we arrived at her father's. The new moon had set, and it was quite dark. I held one of her hands in mine while opening the gate that she might pass through: the impulse was upon me. Conscience raised a voice of warning. Caution pulled its thousand strings. They were nothing. I obeyed the impulse and pressed her hand. Warm and velvety it was,—and something more. The keenest delight I believe my soul has ever experienced, was at that moment. Tenderly given it was—that response—

with a tremor of her fingers. I felt it all. I feel it now. I felt it this evening, when we were sitting in silence, and the twilight was fading. I shall never forget it; for it was the first true love-response that greeted my opening passion.———

"What time is it?" asked the Quaker of the supposed lawyer, who was consulting his watch.

"I beg pardon, sir," responded the other, essaying to put his watch back into its fob. "Don't let it interrupt you. It's impudence I know; but don't let it interrupt you, sir."

"By no means," cheerfully said the Quaker. "I really want to know the time. My watch has stopped."

Assured that he had done no outrage, the lawyer drew forth his time-piece again, and scrutinizing it carefully by the moonlight, he announced that it was quarter-past nine.

"You will release me, then, I hope," said the Quaker, addressing us collectively. "It's bed-time for honest people, according to the saying."

"Yes, but you don't mean to apply that remark to the present company, I hope," remarked the lawyer, facetiously inclined.

No attention was paid to the remark, and the Quaker went on—"I think I've discharged my duty. We were up pretty late last night. By the way, too, here's another gentleman. If you wish further entertainment, he is prepared, no doubt. I mo"——

"None of your motioning," the lawyer put in, promptly. "You're not going to fool us thus. Don't you know, my esteemed friend, that your story's only half done? You have lived thus far in vain, if you suppose we'll let you off this side of eternity without t'other half. I'll leave it to the rest of the company." We assented to the lawyer's remark. After which the bald-headed man observed, there being silence, "I think it's very inter*es*tin'."

"You do? Indeed!" responded the Quaker, smiling; and we all smiled; for the bald-headed was very earnest in his manner. There was more silence. "By the by," said the lawyer, "before you begin again—you've got to begin, sir!—I want to indulge in something personal. Why is it you don't say thee and thou, being a Quaker?"

"When among Romans, be a Roman."

"That's all, is it?"

The Quaker bowed assent, saying, "When I am

away from home I never indulge in things calculated to reveal the social and religious relations in which I have been reared—except as my dress may betoken them." This satisfied the lawyer, and he was apparently about to express his satisfaction, when the Quaker interrupted, asking—"Have I—to return the same coin—have I guessed right in guessing—my Yankee friends will excuse my play upon their favorite word—that you have left the sea, and now practice law?"

"True as the world!" responded the other with some surprise. "There *is* some shrewdness left. I *am*, sir, an humble aspirant to forensic distinction, I am happy to say. But these things are foreign to the case. I suppose now as I've obliged you with a direct answer to a leading question, you will not object to directly taking up the thread of your discourse, eh? Gentlemen, I perceive it in his eye—Listen.

CHAPTER VII.

Obedient to the lawyer's injunction, we listened.

I am sorry—so the Quaker resumed, first addressing the lawyer—that you find it in your heart to be so exacting. I hope you will have occasion to repent. I fear you will. Your abettors, too. Gentlemen, I mean no disrespect;—that man knoweth not what he doth. But to your general selfishness represented in him, I make no appeal; only remarking, that I began with no determined end, but that I begin now, with such end full in view, and you *must* accompany me to it. If it prove a punishment, it will be no more nor less than you deserve. So much; and you may call it preface.

Now, let's see, where did I leave my young self? In great bliss I remember. Yes, at the gate, in a rapturous aberrance, from which he directly recovered sufficiently to mount the carriage and drive home. A sweet, tumultuous overflow of sentiment visited me that night, happifying and beautifying the vista of the future—before I slept, most beamingly—afterwards in gorgeous flashes that thrilled me as one entranced is thrilled with visions of heaven. Adored Fanny! could she but know what that tremulous response had done for me! This was the fervent wish of my heart when I awoke, or rather came out of physical sleep. I did not awake. No; though the dream was troubled, sorely troubled, as with fiends dire and remorseless, I did not awake. I have not awaked; ay, I dream still on that very subject, though I must confess the dream has for many long years seemed marvellously like reality. Pardon this anticipating—this weaving ahead of the main cloth, to use a metaphor. I am no ingenious fictionist. This is my excuse.

I have now a new character to bring before you; and I approach him in the bright field—beyond the intervening shadows—as I would approach a serpent. Samuel Toom. Old Abel's only child. The boy whom Joshua saved from drowning. A handsome boy in shape he was—symmetrically built and easy of movement. To see him at a little distance, walking, one could not help exclaiming at his singularly graceful carriage, and a stranger would have approached him sure of being pleased. Nor would the contemplator have been undeceived until he came to look closely upon his countenance. There the devil within him ever dwelt, sleepily coiled—like an adder. Sleepily coiled, yet within ever nerved to the most deadly precision. I do not speak now as I felt then. I had then a dim eye towards human faces—a charitable way of considering human actions.

This Samuel Toom had been at one short time during my earlier boyhood an intimate; and notwithstanding Joshua's disparaging remarks, I retained an affection for him up to the time of which I shall soon speak. His father being poor, Samuel had been obliged early in life to shift for himself; and he had shifted so much to his advantage that he had at the age of fourteen obtained a situation in a dry-goods store in Harrisburg, nearly seventy miles from his old home—working his way there unaided, except by his own ingenuity and craft. He was about a year older than I, and was therefore at this time in his seventeenth year—just Fanny's age.

I was surprised to meet him at the pic-nic. He

told me after our greeting, which was cordial on my part, that he had returned the week before, and would remain a couple of months—" to," he said whisperingly in my ear, " spark the country gals, you know,—among other things of less importance," he added aloud. I inhaled his breath. It was strong with brandy.

" Thy breath smells bad," said I reprovingly.

" Only a little for the awcasion, you know," he answered with a kind of snorting smirk, and left me, mingling again with the company. From that moment I began to distrust him.

The next evening after the pic-nic Fanny was at our house a little while. While there, she stayed in the sitting-room, and talked in a lively manner with my mother and Cynthia about one thing and another, among the rest mentioning the fact, that her parents had determined to send her to Harrisburg to attend school a year. The announcement startled me, who was listening in rapt attention, into asking her when she intended to go. My voice trembled some, at which my sister smiled, but Fanny was sober, and there was a marked sadness in her tone when she answered, that the intention was to have her go about the first of November. "What! so soon as that!" exclaimed Cynthia, and she, too, was sober. Nothing more was said about it.

That night a comforting determination took possession of me. I would visit Fanny. She was going away, and therefore it could not be improper nor harmful. The recollection of the sweet response, too, confirmed me. Yet I would not be precipitous. Two months must elapse before her departure. I would wait awhile; but I would certainly go—once at any rate.

It was a happy resolution, and in the morning I found myself deepened in it. I at once chose the day upon which I would make the call, and my mind settled down fixedly upon it.

The intervening time was much longer in passing than my imagination had taught me to believe it would be, but the day came at last, and, after elaborate adjustments at the toilet, I sallied forth, without informing any one of my destination. I found Fanny at home, body and soul. She received me cordially, without any appearance of surprise, and behaved towards me something after a sisterly fashion, talking and laughing with exceeding liveliness—too much animation, I thought, to be altogether pleasing. She took me into the garden, and showed me her Autumn-flowers, some of which were fading. One was drooping—the stalk being fractured—and she stooped over it, caressing and propping it. She spoke tenderly of it, and of its being a flower such as Seraph used to love. After that, while I stayed, she was as I wanted her to be. Her voice was plaintive; and just before I went away, she spoke of her anticipated departure, shedding tears.

It was a pleasant interview, all in all, and brought me to another determination, namely, to visit her again, though she had not requested it. That she had not was an inadvertence to me—by a convenient sophistry made to appear—and did not take form as objection to my going again. Precisely two weeks—two weeks was the interval before, dating from my first resolve—and I would repeat the visit. So regular we are before the race becomes desperate!

Two weeks. As a kind of disagreeable necessity they passed—*at length*, being in a manner insupportably dry and uninteresting, except a little ogling—the first—on one of the intervening Sabbaths. A sweet, delicate taste it was, like honey distilled. Oh, that such dews would lull the craving! Then might love abide and be always sweet.

The promised evening came, and equipped in my best, I made the promised visit. With tremendous thumpings of heart, which sounded to me much louder than the bashful knock that I laid upon the door, I stood expectant. She met me all smiles, and overflowing with cheerful remarks—*very* cordial she was, and polite. I did not like it. There seemed a frost in it. But she was less lively after a little, and brought me a book of hers to read—conversation having flagged. A favorite she said, and pointed out several passages, turning over the leaves, while I held the book, with her pretty fingers—there was nothing frosty in that. When she had pointed out the passages, she went away to the window, looking out, while I made a feint of reading. As I was turning over the leaves something fell out of the book upon the floor. I did not pick it up at first; and when I did, in a fit of absence, I put it in my pocket.

I did not stay so long this time as before, but left in a charmed state, determined, even previous to taking leave, that I would come again. Two weeks more. That was to be my last visit, I resolved, and hoped to be able to keep my resolve. But I did not make the visit. The cause will appear.

On the evening fixed, I prepared my exterior with care, as usual, and was about starting, when a succession of trifles sprang up, which so hindered me that I did not start until nearly dark. As I was hurrying along, my mind filled with the honeyed vapor of my anticipations, I was brought to a sudden halt, by hearing a groan, as of one in distress. I immediately saw the source of it—S. Toom. "Samuel what ails thee?" I inquired with solicitude.

"Deacon, is that you? By the Lord, but I'm glad." He was sitting by the road-side, cherishing one of his feet, from which the boot was removed. "What ails thy foot?" I inquired further, guessing that to be the seat of his distress.

"Foot?" he responded, "I have a story to tell you. I hope you'll befriend me, eh? I know you will: you're the likeliest young man in *this* town, and the best friend I've got, too. Well, I was down to the river to-day, on a stroll, and I felt something crawling in my boot. Directly I sits down on the bank-- I was right along there where it's steep, you know. Off comes boot. Nothing in that. Crawl, crawl, in my stocking. I pulls at the stocking like Satan,—scart a little, you understand. I jerked. My stocking came off unexpectedly, and my hand hit the boot—and, by the poker! knocked the thing right off into the river, and away it went. Now the fact is, I've been trying to get home without it, and I'm about dead. My foot—lord! it seems like a blister. Deacon, the fact is, I've got to ask a favor of you, now you're here."

I begged him to name it without reserve—I was in a hurry; but *that* I did not mention. "I know it's an ungraceful request. But I'll be bound to you all my life if you'll accede. The fact is, I want one of your boots for about a half hour or so, till I can cut home and back again. Now do." I had a dim eye towards human faces, and it was dark, too. I let him have my boot.

Half-an hour! I could bear the sacrifice to do an act of kindness. He had incidentally promised to come back there with the boot, and so I sat down whence he had arisen, and waited. It was nearly opposite the gate, and in full view of the parlor windows. Not long after the gentleman had disappeared, and while I was looking and longing, the parlor was suddenly lighted, and the shutters to one of the windows thrown open. I could see in quite distinctly. I saw Fanny, waiting for me, not very impatiently, I guessed, for I heard her laugh aloud, and strike off into a lively remark of some sort—I could almost hear the words—I tried to hear them, be assured, holding my breath. A change took place in the lights, so that I saw in more distinctly, and I saw—I wiped my eyes, and saw standing by the centre-table, a young man. It was no illusion, though I had at first a disposition to make it so. Who was it? Who *was* it? I could almost say for a certainty. I arose to my feet unconsciously, looking—not looking so much as piercing with my eyes; but the distance—jealous distance!—it forbade. I walked across the street: when I reached the fence, I looked again, but he was not to be seen. Fanny had taken a seat by the window, resting her elbow on the sill. There was a masculine arm and hand resting on the same sill. My physical vision of these facts was dim, but my mental—how vivid! Could I have known just then to whom that reposing arm and hand belonged, it might have given me a kind of hangman's relief. But that was not vouchsafed.

I returned to the opposite fence and waited. A half-an hour I knew it was, and yet no boot. A passing suspicion had been in my mind. It came again, passing quickly, however, because I would not have it so. The moon was rising above the trees very brightly. It shone upon that window brighter and brighter. I crossed the street again. I had almost ceased to expect my boot that night, and that suspicion was wrestling sorely with my incredulity. The forms were gone from the window. Directly, I heard voices in the garden—the garden was by the street, a few yards from where I stood. I crept along the fence—crept slower and slower, and lowlier, listening. It was Fanny talking about the moonlight. I heard her words, but I paid little attention to them. I was searching for a greater fact; she ceased speaking, and immediately the fact was developed: "I cannot tell thee how much I love it, too." The self-same voice my boot was begged with!—on a different key—floating with the most winning modulation—but the same. It was as a clap of thunder first, and then as martial music to me. My blood boiled with unutterable rage. It was genuine wrath seven times heated; and it grew hotter with every pulsation of my furious heart. But in the midst of it there was conscience—kind monitor! The All-seeing only knows what the "still, small voice" saved the demon Samuel, that night, perhaps his life. He had trifled with my heart's best impulses, and he was trifling with its sweetest. Conscience! But for that I would have torn him. Yet my mother had not sought to inculcate the spirit of the words, "Turn the other cheek, also," in vain. The general remembrance calmed me like the voice of an angel, and I walked homeward—what need had I longer to stay? pervaded with a sense of something like a triumph. Yet it was to some degree illusive. One strong sentiment had displaced another, and when the reaction came, which was soon, I was thrown into a condition—new then—since more familiar. I was jealous; and all the pangs of that helpless state were mine. I ceased to reflect upon the wrong Samuel had done me, and thought, with a most turbulent incongruity and unreasonableness of feeling, only of Fanny. I do not remember now how I made out the case. But I found plenty of aliment for the new condition, and could not go to sleep even after I heard the clock toll the hour of midnight, and I tried to sleep. The lively laugh, the juxtaposition of the two arms and hands on the window-sill, the pathetic apostrophe to the moonlight, I could recall it clearly—they were in my mind as memories of events vitally important.

They multiplied, and their offspring were more hideous than they. I was tortured, but at last fell asleep.

In the morning, as I was hanging up my fine vest, I saw something white, sticking out of one of the pockets. I plucked it forth. It was a card. There was writing on it:—"Dear Frances, * * * your devoted friend, S. Toom." I looked at it more narrowly. It could not be so bad as that. No; it was only an invitation to attend a pic-nic, the pic-nic of six weeks previous, I saw by the date. The date—it was one day after that of my note to her. Ay, I saw another fact—two of them. She had, before receiving this card, pledged herself to me, otherwise——, and she had slipped this card into my pocket that I might know, and that I might no further interfere. Why, it was as plain as—as—I wanted it to be. "Fear not," said I, addressing a profile view of her in my imagination, "I pity thee·

but I will not disturb thy short-lived happiness," and in a resigned mood I went down to breakfast.

The next evening but one, I was sitting on the front-door step by myself. The sky was overcast, and the dismal autumn-wind howled and moaned in the forest, and whistled mysteriously about the old house. The wind was not cold, but especially sad in its tone, whether from wandering far among bare boughs and withered leaves and dry stalks that had once borne flowers, I know not, perhaps—and perhaps a deeper cause—a cause which man would not bear to know in this rudimental state of being—made it so sad. It matters, however, only to know that its wild voice led my soul resistlessly as it had been passionate music. I was very wretched, yet had a kind of glory in my wretchedness. My scope of thought and fancy was not broad, however; and I was buffetted with repetitions which, as they were familiar, had no alleviation. I was getting into deep despondency—almost to tears, when, hearing a slight rustling sound in the direction of the street, I looked up, just in time to see my honest, ill-used boot come swooping over the front fence straight towards me. End over end it came, descending, and, striking flat on the paved path, slid up to my very feet, the leg thereof lopping towards me like a clumsy bow. It was nearly dark, yet I could see, as I picked up the boot, a roughly sketched figure on the face of it—a representation of a thumb, a nose, and fingers to correspond. I took the idea. It stabbed me as though it had been a poniard, driven by the same remorseless hand. It was the last, unkindest cut, mangling, annihilating cut. It bewildered me. I could not think of it. I could think of nothing. I went up to my bed, and essayed to lose my woes in sleep. I tried in vain. I could not go to sleep. On the contrary I went wide awake, my mind jerked here and there like a piece of bread in a nest of ants. I tossed until I was tired, and then lay still till I was tired. I tossed again, and lay still again, with the same result. There was something wanting that would have made me calm, or something existing within me, originating in myself, which some action of mine could have removed, that made me so restless. The gratuitous cruelty which had been inflicted upon me, could not alone have done it. I felt this fact dimly, as one asleep feels external things—then more distinctly, awakening. Perhaps my suspicion regarding

Fanny was unfounded. A recollection flashed upon me. That card I had put in my own pocket. It fell from her book. Shameful, shameful, that I should ever have thought it. Fanny was just as lively in her bearing towards me, as I had seen her that night towards Samuel. It was her habit. Sam would not have taken such pains to impose upon me, had he been sure of his prize. Thus a new view dawned upon my judgment, and I saw why I was so restless. I had wronged Fanny; yet only in my heart. I grew calm speedily, and was soon asleep.

In the morning I awoke in the same calm state of mind in which I had fallen asleep. I remembered Samuel's unmannerly deed; but reflected coolly upon it; for I had assurance that it was a dastardly act, which would come out at his cost.

The day of Fanny's departure came. I had been once in the meantime to see her; but had not found her at home. The friendly, and slightly regretful allusion she had made to it a day or two after at our house, where she had called a few minutes, I dared to conjecture, chiefly to express her regret, atoned fully for the disappointment, and I meditated upon her anticipated departure with unmingled sorrow.

The day came. My sister and I were there. Few words were spoken. Her father, mother and brother were to accompany her; so she had only to bid farewell to Cynthia and me. As we all stood at the gate—the carriage being in readiness, and she but a minute to stay—she took us both at once by the hand, and touching her lips to Cynthia's, said, with deep earnestness.

"I do not like to leave you. I know I shall find no friends so good. Do thou write to me Cynthia—often. Good-by!"

We made no response. Cynthia was weeping, and I was little short of it.

"Good-by!" she said again, after mounting the carriage. We gave back the word mechanically, and turned away to our home very sorrowful.

For a few days I was very sad. But I gradually got the better of it, though visited with occasional pangs from the consciousness that Samuel would be near her, he having returned to Harrisburg a few days before she went.

I resumed my attendance at the village school, and in the pursuit of my studies lost sight, in a measure, of my social afflictions. The days passed pleasantly.

and the nights—with exceptions. I was cheerful and hopeful.

Some time about midwinter, one evening, as I was sitting with the family, my mother interrupted the silence, addressing my father—"Ahasuerus, hast thou thought on that matter?"

"Yes, yes," responded my father, testily.

"Well," said my mother, and there was silence again.

My curiosity was awakened, and I waited for something further. Presently, after much fumbling in and about his pockets, my father went to the bureau and brought a letter. "From Joshua," whispered Cynthia to me.

"Deacon," said my father, seating himself, "what does thee think about it?" I did not know what he meant, and told him so. "Read the letter to him," said my mother. My father, thereupon, read it—slowly through his spectacles—until he came to the last page. I could see nothing especial in it, and I remarked to that effect, interrupting my father. "Wait, my son," observed my mother, significantly.

"Your son, Ahasuerus the younger," read my father; "a word or so or more about him. I like the boy, and it has occurred to me that he is not altogether contented with his present prospects for the future. I want to see the lad brought out, and properly harnessed for the battle. Now I have to propose, in so many words, that the boy come here and study medicine with me."

"That's *it*," remarked my father. "Now, what does thee think of it?"

I had but one thought of it. "Of course, I'll go," said I.

"Thou must think seriously on it, my son," enjoined my mother. "It is for life." So I knew, and it strengthened my sudden resolve. "I'll go," said I again. "I don't see as there's anything more to be said about it, then," observed my father, appealing to my mother. "Nothing now," she replied soberly.

Glorious, new future to me! The old was cast off as filthy rags, and in the warmth of my imagination, I longed to start upon the new path—even that night.

In a few days the matter was, after various earnest consultations, arranged. It was determined that I should remain at school until it should close; and thereafter immediately go to Harrisburg to commence my medical studies.

The winter wore away. The spring came. The school closed, and I set about preparing for departure. It was a grievous trial for my parents and Cynthia to part with me, and there was much weeping and heaviness of heart on the morning that I went away. Delia was there with her child, a healthful, lively little creature, who called me by the same nick-name—because it couldn't pronounce the whole name—by which Seraph used to call me. They all gathered around me at the old gate, all feeling very sad—all except father and little Isaac, the baby. They were exceptions, because father was going with me, and little Isaac wouldn't be anything else; and his lively example exercised considerable counteracting influence, so that the actual moment of parting was more cheerful than otherwise.

We walked over to the village—my father and I—my trunk having been sent earlier in the morning by the hired-man. At the village we took stage, and late in the night drove into the city of Harrisburg. By pre-arrangement we stopped at the hotel where Joshua boarded, and in the morning, as we descended to breakfast, we met him in the lower hall. "Unexpectedly fortunate all through life;"—thus he began, before we saw him, his voice sounding like a familiar tune; then taking our hands, he inquired about our condition of body and mind, and about that of those at home, coming to a dead stop when my father incidentally mentioned the infant Isaac, declaring, with an excellent imitation of sudden physical debility, that he *must* have breakfast immediately, or perish under the stroke.

At the table he so far recovered as to remark that it had become imperatively necessary for him to keep better note of the passage of time. "Why," said he, "it seems but yesterday, or the day before, at most, that Delia was a handsome, promising female babe; and now you say a being actually exists that calls her mother! It was bad enough to have her married before I could realize the absence of her short clothes. But now—you're a veracious man, and have a boy, here, who bears an oath in his countenance to confirm your statement. I must give in, I suppose."

After breakfast, he conducted us to his office, which I entered with a feeling somewhat akin to awe

But that feeling passed off in a measure, soon—sufficiently to allow my entering into a survey of the premises. While my father and Joshua were indulging in some reminiscent observations, I went on with my survey. The office comprised two rooms—the front one being furnished with a set of plain chairs, much worn—the more so, I thought then, shrewdly, for having been so often occupied by nervous invalids; a round table, covered with green baize, worn through in several places, particularly within elbow-reach of the front edge; an old desk—very old—in which were many—it seemed to me then innumerable—phials, of every possible variety of shape and size; a stove—but that was bran new, which fact I inferred as much as anything from its having been spit upon but twice—at least, had but two stains of tobacco juice upon it; and last of all, a pile of books lying on the round table. I noticed these last in order, and went to them for a closer scrutiny. They were, or purported to be, "Collections from the Old Masters." Music, all music; not a word of printing as I could see, except the title-pages. Two of them were ponderous volumes—huge quartos, bound in thick sheep-skin. The others were smaller—contents arranged for the voice. In *them* was something that at first sight looked like printing; but I could make no sense of it, so I concluded it was musical signs, and was about expressing myself on the subject, when Joshua remarked, parenthetically to what he was saying to my father, "Careful, my boy. Those books are the apple of mine eye." This embarrassed me so much that I immediately gave up the investigation, and took a seat, gathering assurance again by looking into the back-room. That room was carpeted, and the windows shaded with red curtains. It had a plain, neat settee in it, and an interminable library—so my impression was then—of books old and new, with gilt-lettered titles, written titles, and no titles. Some of them were not bound, some with one side-cover on; some in cloth, some in paper, others in leather—heavy leather and fine leather, polished. Some very large and thick, some large and thin, some small and worn as with much handling. Immense the number seemed. If I had been required to guess it, I presume I should have said ten thousand, feeling safe; though in fact there were not more than three hundred. As I looked I became interested, for that was the pile in whose labyrinths I was to wander for the next half a dozen years. I went into the room to take a narrower look. My former ideas were only magnified. I became bewildered directly, and tired, and was glad to retreat from the solid, august array. I retreated, back foremost, stumbling over a chair as I re-entered the front room, which mishap aroused Joshua and my father, who were deep down in some well, groping for reluctant facts that had once been living truths to them—aroused them very much, and they both stretched and yawned into a full realization of the present. "The time, Joshua?" asked my father.

"The time"—began Joshua, musingly. "Oh, the time of day?" he continued, drawing forth his watch, and suppressing a laugh at his misapprehension. "Why, you've been here about an hour." He then stated the hour, whereupon my father jumped up as though casting off a burden, or by the motion was extracting one of his teeth, and declared he must be at the hotel in half an hour, that he might not be left behind. Joshua apprehended him at first, with some real difficulty, and afterwards with much sham. And when the idea that my father was to return home that day, was fully developed in his mind, he beset him in the most vigorous manner, to treat the intention, as *he* did, with unmeasured contempt. But my father was inflexible, and we all went back to the hotel.

Just before the stage drove up, my father took Joshua one side, and talked in a low, serious voice to him. I could see their faces; and I saw that Joshua took what was said with calm, serious assent, and that my father was singularly earnest. I guessed the theme, though I could not distinguish a word, and I felt a kind of glory in having two such protectors in this world.

Soon the stage drove up, and my father, taking my hand, said very mechanically, with his voice pitched on an unusual key, "Good-by!" It was all he said; and I'm inclined to think all he could say, and maintain his dignity. He did not look at me any more, but took his seat stiffly, and passed away from our presence, gazing steadfastly into the fore-interior of the stage.

Home had so far seemed connected with me; but now that connection was severed—the cord was winding up away from me, and I felt for the moment quite alone. A great sigh was preparing to escape me, when was I brought to a healthful and proper sense of my real position, by Joshua taking me by the arm, and leading me off with mock severity, towards his office.

"I hope," said he, keeping up the joke, as he went along, "that your behavior will be such, that extremities will not have to be resorted to. Be calm, sir, and in due time you will be released, a better and a wiser man."

When we reached the office, he changed his tone, saying, "Deacon, for a day or two, wander and sip, and get so you can look around without staring. Then I'll begin with you—yea, I will put you upon the tread-wheel; but you shall have oats, and a prospect of meadows green, where streams perennial flow, and where sweet wild oats grow, you know."

I made a remark, embodying my impressions of the place, to which he responded, "Just so. May you always be happy, bedewed, and refreshed for ever in this world of woe!—By the way, Deacon, I must go out professionally. Tell any one who enters the premises, that you can't do anything for them; and that Doctor Noyles is gone out." So saying, he left me alone, to amuse myself till noon.

What do you suppose I thought of, the very first

thing after Joshua went out, and the room was silent. Just this:—Fanny Cline. I thought of her, and I thought not seriously of anything else all the time Joshua was gone—more than two hours. I thought warm thoughts, and cool thoughts—warm thoughts of her, of *her*, living, adorable angel! and cool thoughts of a plan by which I would gain an interview with her. Nothing came of it, however, but a nervous head-ache, which lasted, getting severer towards night, until I fell asleep—late in the evening.

The next morning I kept such thoughts out of my mind by special edict of the will, and commenced seriously to reconnoitre the awful library. But before the close of the day—it was near the close—when I thought I had done all that an attempt required; I took a seat facing one of the windows in the back room, which window opened towards the west, and I became enthralled again, as I had been the day before. The window was up, and the curtain, and I watched the great, red sun, as it went calmly down, not thinking about it, but about what it suggested. The same sun, looking nearly the same, had gone down another season, shining in my face, while my ear drank the pathetic melody of that mild voice so thrillingly sweet—then. When the sun was down, there was a soft flush of living twilight. And I made it still more alive, for I was so fanciful as to weave a bright angelic form there, in the midst of it. But it was a fleeting form, only suggesting thoughts that made me indifferent to the twilight. A lively train. She is in the same city with me, and we are away from home—so the train moved. She is sitting perhaps at this moment, at the western window of her room—her own private room, thinking. Thinking! oh, that I were there, to help her think—to talk with her—about home. Oh, I would not talk with her about anything else. Only about home. Perhaps about the pic-nic, as being legitimately connected with it. Perhaps about the evening that followed. No; I would not allude to that. She might, if she wished. I hope she will. The morning in the spring, too, when thou and Cynthia came out into the field where I was. That was home. We will talk about that, sweet Fanny. Hold! ahem! It was of no use. I had been talking aloud—two or three sentences. Is it possible any one?——— There was Joshua's face, resting against the door-casing, looking solemnly at me.

"My dear boy," said he, with much feeling, instead of laughing, as I anticipated, "I beg your pardon sincerely. Some day you may know why I stood here and listened. Not now." He came in, and put his arm around me as a tender father would around a son younger than I was, and said, in a livelier tone, "Deacon, the world looks bright to you now, don't it?" Overcome with embarrassment at the disclosure I had made, I replied "yes," without meaning it. Whereupon, he patted my shoulder, saying, "To-morrow it won't look so bright; for I'm going to begin to endow you with my mantle of wisdom, with the help of Providence, and these books here." Thus the subject was entirely changed. And it continued changed; for directly afterwards, a crony of Joshua's came in, and they sat down, spending the evening after a manner which did not afford opportunity for quiet—or much other—thought. This crony was afflicted in like manner with Joshua, namely, taking an overwhelming pleasure in music, accompanied with the bald illusion that he could make it. The evening was spent dreadfully, if we may attach any sacredness to the splendid creations of the "Old Masters," and tired at beholding the conflict, I slipped off, while the stimulated actors were executing a flanking measure to save themselves in the heights of a solo, and went away to my bed anticipating a renewal of the twilight reflections; but I suddenly and unexpectedly fell asleep.

The following morning my studies were commenced in earnest, and with them commenced a new and deep interest, which to this day has never ceased. But that interest, deep and lively as it was, and daily increasing, did not engross me. At quiet closes of day, and sometimes at other quiet hours when I was alone in the office, thoughts that were not of science, hopes that were not of distinction, gave light and life to my inner soul. And the more they came, the more they glowed, and the more I longed to see with my bodily vision the object of them.

One evening—Sunday evening—I think it was the fourth Sunday of my sojourn—the mood was strong upon me; and in three minutes from the time the plan commenced, it was formed, and the day appointed upon which I would go and see her—Fanny. The principal part of the plan was to inform Joshua of my intention, and ask his advice. This was done modestly in the dark, as we were walking that same evening. I stated that she was an old friend of mine, and that I wanted to see her very much, and so forth, and so on—concealing the main fact as though he didn't know it—and concluded with naming the day I had conditionally appointed. The whole matter was rather awkwardly and incoherently stated, and he pretended not to understand, requesting me to repeat, which I did; and in my anxiety to be explicit, I got so near the true state of the case that I told it bolt out, which I have no doubt was just what he wanted, for he met my confession with another embrace like the one of that second evening of my stay, and tendered at once his entire services. He had two or three patients, he said, in the institution, and was well acquainted with the teachers. He would go with me, and give me an introduction. Thus the matter was briefly arranged.

Friday—the day came, and we went together as agreed. I was introduced first to the principal, a bland, amiable-appearing man, and afterwards by him to a manly-looking person in woman's clothes, who wore spectacles over very severe, pale-blue eyes. Fanny was under her immediate supervision, she informed me, with very distinctly accented phraseology, and through her, as a gate, I was admitted to the ambrosial presence. I had seen the dear being only in memory and imagination for the past five or six months, yet I knew her step before she entered the room, and I arose all aglow to greet her. But the gate creaked. "Ahem!" significantly remarked the manly-looking in woman's clothes. Fanny was all aglow, too; but that "ahem?" was magically chilling in its effect. She came demurely up to me, and just touched my fingers with hers, and then took a seat on the opposite side of the room. A stiff dialogue thereupon ensued relative to home, and present prospects, likes and dislikes, intentions and so forth, and thus a half an hour passed—to me as something sweet, swallowed whole; and I went away with a feeling of dissatisfaction, which I communicated to Joshua as we proceeded together towards the office.

"All natural and inevitable," he observed, "but it's no use to fret. Wait for a more propitious sky, and other more propitious circumstances." He further remarked, that the school would be out early in the summer, and left the subject for me to pursue.

It was a very consoling thought to me that a vaca

tion was so soon to ensue in Fanny's school, and I at once embraced a plan of action. It was plain, I reflected, that I could not visit her again as she was then situated, with any satisfaction, consequently I would defer all until the vacation. Then, before she should return, I would gain the sweet opportunity. To this end I immediately dispatched a billet by post, signifying my desire. To my agreeable surprise, I received an answer the day following, briefly granting my request. It was written evidently in great haste—so I concluded by way of explanation of the facts that the hand-writing only resembled hers, and that two or three words were misspelled, a fault which in all her long letters to Cynthia I had never noticed. But I was too happy in my success to reflect nicely upon these things, and accordingly put the billet away, gratefully settling down upon the promised joy.

Six weeks were to elapse before vacation would commence, and to the consumption, by the inch, of the long dreary interval, I addressed myself. Yet it was not so dreary when I got fairly at it, and four of the six weeks were soon past. I specify thus, for at the end of those four weeks, an event happened.

Since my arrival in Harrisburg, I had not seen S. Toom, though I had thought of him—and that not tenderly—often. Neither did I want to see him. But it was otherwise ordered. I was sitting one morning in the office-door, pleasantly reflecting upon the fact, that two-thirds of the hindrance to the anticipated interview were removed, when "Good morning, Doctor Munn," startled me like a hiss. I looked up savagely, and there he stood, most deferentially, with his hat off. "Worthy disciple of Esculapius, how do you do this morning?" he continued, perceiving I was not likely to return his salutation. I said nothing, and looked perseveringly away from him. But he was far from being bluffed. He ran on to considerable length in a very lively, desultory discourse upon the medical practice, old times, future times, present times, and local matters, and coming to an emphatic conclusion by asking me what were the latest advices from the Cline family. Boiling with wrath, I only looked fiercely in his face. "They say Fanny is in the city at school," he continued, his sleepy, serpent eyes nearly closed. "Demned squash-head of a girl, I think, eh? Time thrown away schooling her." I knew this was meant to insult me, and I resented it by leaving him, and going into the back-room. "Well, Doctor," I heard him say, standing at the door, "I suppose thou wouldst not take a little something to drink this morning—a little cold water toddy?" It was too much. Grasping a pestle, I rushed out, angry, even to the shedding of blood. But he was gone. I was yet rushing towards the door, when Joshua presented himself, having just returned from a professional call. "Ay! ay! what's this," he began. "Sam Toom, the wretch!" I foamingly ejaculated. "Ah," he responded, becoming very gloomy in an instant, and said nothing more. "What shall I do?" I cried, seeing that I could take no revenge. "Kill him. Kill him," replied Joshua, the veins standing out like cords on his forehead. The next moment he remarked, "I didn't mean that, Deacon. Don't shed blood."

I was greatly agitated, and it was several hours before I regained my mental equilibrium.

Such was the event; and it prepared me to appreciate what followed.

The promised day came. It was Monday—the school having closed on Saturday. At the appointed hour—three in the afternoon—I went. I passed through the same process that I had before, only that I introduced *myself* to the bland principal, who introduced me to the manly-looking with spectacles. "Sir?" said she when I inquired for Fanny. I repeated. "Frances is no longer under my immediate supervision," she informed me with admirable accentuation. That I knew; but perhaps she could tell me where Fanny was, that I might see her. "Sir?" What a voice of thunder! I repeated more explicitly and emphatically. Worse than ten thousand thunders was that voice to me, when she said—"Frances is gone out to walk with an old acquaintance of hers. Toom I think was the name by which he was introduced to me. She will be in towards evening. Please to call again." In other words—please to clear out. So I took her request, at least, and went away, away from the house, from the heavenly dream that had so long made me happy—-away down, down. Oh, the blackness of darkness! the worse than sulphureous depths into which I was plunged!

It would be but mockery to attempt a description of my feelings during the rest of that afternoon and evening—all that night, in fact, for I did not sleep. Jealousy and hate in all their burning fury, tore me as vultures would have torn. At one moment Fanny would appear to me a ruined creature, fascinated by the remorseless serpent.—The next moment she would appear a deceitful hag, hateful beyond expression. Toom—I could not think of him—it was too frenzying.

It was a dreadful tumult all through the long night; and in the morning I showed traces of it too plainly to attempt concealment. I told Joshua about it—keeping nothing back. His only reply was "Wait. Let time prove." But that was a branch of practical philosophy which I had not then come to; accordingly I settled my mind at once, or tried to,—coming after several hours reflection, to the conclusion, that Fanny was the one to blame—that she had maliciously deceived and wronged me. And with this conclusion, I settled down quite stolidly, feasting upon my future revenge, which was to commence with a full disclosure to Cynthia, accompanied with appropriate reflections—intended, you know, for Fanny's perusal, as she would be at home.

Having thus settled my plan, I was prepared to dismiss the subject, which was not easily done—was not done at all, in fact. I directly found that when not actively employed at something else pleasingly interesting, my mind would recur in spite of me to the unhappy event. Neither would my thirst for vengeance allow me to rest. The scathing epistle was elaborately inscribed with many tremendous gushes of feeling indicated by gnashings of teeth and smitings with the clenched hand. Some *very* bitter sentences were penned, and underscored with three and some with four lines; and all, being duly complete, was *sent*.

After this fiery transaction I was more at rest, yet had a secret panting for an answer. I was sure of getting one. I was sure Cynthia would sympathize with me, and hasten to make it known. I waited, waited. No letter came for a long time. I received one from my mother first,—then some time after—in all more than four weeks from the sending of mine—one from Cynthia, in which not the slightest allusion was made to the interesting theme. She stated casually that *my old friend* Fanny was in feeble health, and would not probably return to her school, and stated in postscript that S. Toom was at home, dangerously sick. She had received my letter, for she acknowledged it. "Let 'em die together, and Cynthia with 'em, confound her," said I, pinching the innocent letter, and flapping it against the r... d table. I was alone in my misery. My own dear sister was willing to sacrifice her only brother, and encourage a deluded girl—so I viewed it just then—to utter destruction. Who was ever so unhappy as I was then? Yet I had consolations. I took hold of my studies vigorously, and they diverted me. I leaned more on Joshua, though I didn't mention the subject to him—and he diverted me. I learned to laugh at the frequent musical catastrophes which transpired in the office, and they diverted me With all, I had after a few days only an hour or so now and then, of dismal thoughts. Thus the summer passed slowly on, even to the end, and autumn commenced. In the meantime I had received several letters from home, from which I gathered two important facts: that Fanny, though well, would no more come back to school; and that Samuel had recovered and left the place.

When the leaves began to fall, I took it into my head to go home and make a visit. Joshua approved of my intention, and I set out early one quiet morning, and after a very pleasant journey, came, just at dark, into the old village. I was there joined by my father, and went home to the old house. As we came to the gate, my mother, Cynthia, and— Fanny, stood there to welcome me. Fanny kept back at first — ay, she remembered my letter, I thought; but in the gush of joy which prevailed, I left that out of mind, and greeted her cordially. Her hand trembled as I held it, and her voice trembled as she asked me, a minute afterwards, gratuitously, if I was well. I had those things to think of that night before I slept.

My visit was to be two weeks in length, and I went at it systematically. The weather was pleasant, and when tired with conversation in the house I wandered out, dreamily renewing the innumerable associations which sprang as echoes from every haunt. I did not tire of these; but there was a sense of dissatisfaction attending them, the source of which I was several days finding out. Fanny was, and yet was not, in everything. I knew it at last, and then everything seemed to reproach me. I remembered her manner the evening that I came home. I remembered what I thought and how I felt when I was in my room that night, and all was still. I remembered these things one quiet, hazy afternoon, sitting at the window of Cynthia's room, looking out towards Mr. Cline's house. I saw Fanny sitting at the parlor window—at least I thought it was she—and at once I had a strong impulse to go and visit her. I was sure—very sure she wanted to see me, and with a decision as sudden as the impulse I determined to go.

It was a most beautiful afternoon, and I strove to realize it more fully as I went along. I went slowly through the gate, gathering internal composure by gazing around in a general way, and sauntered up to the window. It was Fanny sitting there, and she was alone. She requested me to walk in. But I preferred standing outside, so she leaned slightly out of the window, and we talked there together quietly for a while about nothing in particular. She was very calm and earnest in her manner, and looked at my lips and not at my eyes when I spoke. I noticed this, and her earnestness as something unusual, and I began to feel a dearth of items to talk about. A little fountain (pent) sprung loose in my heart. I heard what she said—the sound of her voice—not much more, for I was thinking—I could not help thinking—of the evening of the pic-nic. The tone of her voice was the same as then—more tenderly melodious. That fountain gushed fresher and fuller in my heart, and I felt more barren of items. I became quite absent, and did not hear a question which she casually asked me. "Ahasuerus!" Oh, my name! how sweetly spoken! The fountain was becoming a tide. "Fanny!" I returned. "Come in, Ahasuerus," she said in the same tone; "thou must be tired standing."

I was not tired, but I went in. She bade me be seated on the settee, while she took the rocking-chair, a little distance off.

"Didst thou not ask me something just before I came in?" I inquired, feeling I must make some remark.

"I don't mind, now," she replied, and for several minutes nothing was said.

There was something painful on her mind—something that sought utterance, yet was vigorously kept back.

"Why dost thou look so sad?" I inquired, painfully moved, myself.

"Do not ask me," she replied. Then, after a few moments, continued with a quivering voice, "I have suffered"——

"On my"——account, I was going to say, but I swallowed it, feeling that I need not ask, for it was so. Ay, I knew it. She was weeping.

"Dear Fanny!"

It was the first time, and I was startled at my rashness. But the tide had become an ocean, and bore me resistlessly. I arose and approached her. "My dear Fanny, thou hast suffered by my folly. I am a fool, a detestable fool! I have been a fool all my days, Fanny!"

"Don't talk so, Ahasuerus. Thou art not bad. I am bad. But I can't help it."

I took a chair and sat down beside her—agitated very much. I tried to say several things before I said anything. Finally,—she had ceased weeping, and was looking dreamily away out of the open window—I said, sighed, uttered some way—it was like jumping off a precipice into a bank of tinted clouds—yieldingly I gave it forth, casting all upon the flaming die, "Fanny, my angel!"—a sigh bore the rest—"dost thou love me?"

Her hand was upon mine. She turned her face gently towards mine. I bent towards her. She leaned towards me. Our lips met—our souls met in one long draught of frenzying sweetness.

Unexpectedly as this whole scene had developed itself, I realized it fully in all its vital relations to me. The long-coveted, long-dreamed of treasure was mine, mine. I called her mine, holding her in my embrace —we were then sitting on the sofa. "Yes, Ahasuerus, thine—for ever." How it thrilled me! that word "for ever," spoken so earnestly, as she looked up into my face—into my eyes, now—deep into my soul. We remained silent awhile. Suddenly a dark memory touched me as with shadowy fingers. Samuel. I uttered the name almost involuntarily, so vivid was the remembrance.

"Don't speak of him, he's bad—a bad young man," she said. After a few moments she resumed, "He's unhappy, too. I will show thee something he wrote to me last summer." She arose and went into another room, coming back soon with a letter in her hand. She gave it to me, telling me to read and then destroy it. She had only kept it for me. I read it eagerly, trembling as I read, for I saw therein more than ever the exceeding subtlety and power he possessed. And I saw, too, that it was not all an ingenious play of thoughts. There was true passion in it—burning, deep, and that developed his mental resources—might develop them more! I felt a chill in my blood when I had finished the perusal, as though I had been handling a serpent.

"Dost thou not think he is unhappy?" Fanny inquired, when she saw I was done.

I could not say what I wanted to, so I made no reply.

"He has been bad to thee, I know," she remarked, and there was something unpleasant to me in her manner. I coolly asked, "How?" In reply she entered upon a narration of the event which had given me such poignant misery. Thus it was. She had never received a note from me while at school. Samuel had come there to the institution with a young gentleman and lady of his acquaintance, and begged her to go with him and them to see a floral exhibition, not far off. She had accompanied them, and so the unhappy incident had come to pass.

"Scoundrel!" I could not restrain myself from saying.

"Yes, I know he is bad. We will not say anything more about him."

The sun was down, and the sky overcast thickly, darkly, as I walked home that evening. With all the sweet remembrance of the afternoon, I was not happy.

The following week I returned to Harrisburg, and resumed my studies, immeasurably more buoyant in soul, more vigorous in intellect, than I had left them. The future, how strangely altered from the dark and doubtful to the glorious and certain! There was a cloud, but it was a cloud on the horizon, and did not obscure the day.

The moaning autumn found no echo in my heart, nor did the blustering winter, that came on speedily, congeal my high ardor. My twilight hours were now consumed to a purpose. I committed my gorgeous fancies, my burning thoughts, the voice of my high hopes, to paper; and as the frail bulk accumulated, I sent it away from time to time, to the object upon which they all centered. Responses came, at intervals—far too long intervals in my judgment—tender, precious responses, like that answer she gave when I bent towards her and she leaned towards me, only angels witnessing.

Months passed on. The spring came; the summer—a year went on its way. I again visited home, staying there a month. I saw Fanny twice—had two long interviews with her. At the close of the second, and just as I was leaving her, she gave me two letters, bidding me, as she had at another time, to read, and then destroy them. I read them a few hours after, and with a kind of dread consigned them to flames. They burnt as though alive, and their very ashes, quivering upon the coals, appeared as fiendish ghosts, vengeful at the destruction. Such passion as there was in those letters, so fiery in its voice, so earnest, even in its subtlety,—it seemed in burning them, I was burning the soul that had given them being. Poor Samuel! He *was* unhappy. What might that unhappiness, heightened into despair, not do? I could not dwell upon it.

Again I was at my studies, rapidly progressing in rudimentary acquirement. Another year passed. The stilts of great boyhood were wearing off, and I was getting to be a man. My beard—a shadow cast before—made a modest *débût*, attesting to my having achieved my growth, as well as to the proximity of manhood; and my imagination, fired with the indication, led me, as usual, prematurely into the estate. But it did no harm. I was not of a disposition to take undue advantages of any position, real or supposed, and hence cherished my new-blown dignity rather in secret.

I had in fact grown much older when I visited home this time; but I found the year had been quite general in its effect. My father and mother looked older, and Cynthia, too—a maiden still. Fanny was not older, but riper, less girlish. It was during this visit that I revealed to Cynthia the relation I sustained to Fanny—revealed it, and found it was an old fact to her! This time, too, I talked more of practical affairs with my adored; speaking of the time when she should be my wife, and we should go out hand in hand to meet the rough world. Her reply was like the first. What had words to do with it?

My studies were resumed again, and time passed smoothly, swiftly.

You may wonder I did not again meet with Samuel. He was not in Harrisburg. He was in Boston—had gone there the autumn after his illness, and up to this time had not been back. So Cynthia had told me at my last visit, and she had gathered her information from a conversation between old Abel and my father, which she had overheard. He had not written to Fanny during the year past, which I was more happy to know, than I would have been willing to acknowledge. The only cloud had gone out of my sky.

Time passed smoothly, swiftly. Another year came round. I did not make my annual visit, for at the usual season I was particularly engaged, and afterwards I thought I would wait till spring. I felt the need of it less for having seen all our folks at the city, whither they had come mainly to visit Joshua, they said, and scold him for not having fulfilled his promise of coming out there. Joshua was thunderstruck at the recollection of his promise; but directly took refuge under the sophistry that he had not promised to come in person, and he hoped they had found no fault with his proxy—meaning me. Yet he concluded finally with a direct pledge that he would be with them for a season, about one year from that time.

Spring came; but I did not go then. Joshua was going in the autumn; I was very busy; six months would finish my course, and then I could remain at home half a year if I wished; a long absence would only add sweetness to the meeting. Such were the considerations which determined me not to go. But I repented me soon after; for early in the summer I received a letter from Cynthia, stating, among other facts of interest, that Samuel had been there, remaining more than three weeks, and had called twice on Fanny; and to heighten the effect of this detestable intelligence, I read about the same time a long letter from Fanny herself, in which I found no allusion to Samuel nor his visits. I was wretchedly impatient. But the die was cast.

At last the appointed time arrived, and we—Joshua and I—went. It was late in the season—almost winter; but we had a pleasant journey, rich in small incident, turned to account. Joshua was in the best of good humors all day; and the flow was only freshened on our coming to the old, familiar mansion. Though it was past ten o'clock when we arrived, and we called the inmates out of warm beds, there was no lack of cordiality, and we all sat up, nor was bed alluded to till nearly three in the morning.

I was not long in making my appearance before the idol of my heart. It was the third day, and I was with her several hours—blessed hours, without bitterness. She told me about Samuel in such a way that I was satisfied with her; but my old dread was no way lessened. Ah! no.

I have thus hurried over several years of my life—leaving out much that I would like to have told—in order that I may dwell more minutely upon what followed. Bear with me awhile longer, and I will relate it to you. I had been at home two weeks, perhaps a day or two more, when one afternoon, on returning from a short excursion by myself, I found the family, with Joshua, gathered around the sitting-room fire, apparently in a close consultation, which I interrupted by my entrance. Discovering that they would not resume while I was present, I went out again. In about an hour I returned and was immediately beset by Joshua.

"Young Deacon Ahasuerus Munn, sir. In conclave it has been considered, in conclave it has been decided; amen. Listen! The treasures of your native land have been lavished upon you. The most distinguished and dishonored representative of the Science to which you have devoted yourself—meaning the speaker—has exhausted his resources upon you. Others less dishonored, have been exhausted in rendering assistance, and now it is finished. In view of these facts, sir, it has been decided in conclave that—now, Deacon, it is a serious matter, more serious than it will at first appear to you, and *very* serious to the rest of us, and we have a secret hope you will not consent. It is nothing more nor less than to have you go to Europe, and see if you can learn something that you would not be likely to learn here. I know you are young; but if you wait till you are married, you never *will* go, and so will end another hope of mine. Now say yes, or no, or nothing, eh? How do you like the idea?"

To Europe! The idea was as unexpected as it was overwhelming, and I laughed incredulously.

"No forsaken babes were ever more sincere in their vocal demands than we are in ours," said Joshua. "Will you go, or not?"

"You press rather close," said I in reply. "You" —I had fallen into a temporary habit of modern address, being so much with Joshua—"had no need of asking my consent to this thing. You might with the utmost safety presupposed it."

"So I feared," observed Joshua. "And now let us drop the subject for the present."

The first thing after getting accustomed to the glorious idea, was to communicate it to Fanny, of course. Before I did it, however, the time of departure had been fixed, and sundry other general arrangements had been made. I was to start on the first of April following, and was to remain one year. I broke the intelligence—literally smashed it—to Fanny—for I was too full to allow circumlocution. She received it quite calmly at first, but directly afterwards exhibited more feeling than I had anticipated. It seemed to crush her exceedingly. It was not ordinary grief so much as deep dread that possessed her. I thought it unreasonable, and told her so—gently. She made no reply, and I regretted my remark, seeing that it deepened her depression, and sought to divert her by dwelling upon the advantages I should reap from the tour; the pleasure I should derive; the joy of the future meeting after which there would be no separation till death—dwelling emphatically upon the short time I should be gone. "Only a year," I concluded, trying to look encouraging, not altogether with success, I fear, for her unaccountable feeling had begun to affect me slightly. I felt the mysterious influence more when she said in reply, looking sorrowfully into my face—there was terror, too, in the look—and speaking as though partly to herself: "A year is a great while—a great while. Till thou come back? Yes; I shall live. I feel strangely. I know thou wilt come back. I don't know why I feel so. If I could die when thou goest away. I would rather die. O, Ahasuerus, I am so unhappy!"

I was very unhappy myself after she said this, and for the moment had more than half a thought of revoking my determination. Yet when I went home, and took counsel of my better judgment, I resolved to treat the strange exhibition as a trifle which she would join with me in laughing at on some future day. In this, I succeeded until I saw her again in private. It was the day after Joshua's departure—which happened at the expiration of six very pleasant weeks—and I had a long interview with her—painful, and discouraging. She saw that her state of mind was a source of unhappiness to me, and promised not to indulge in it. I left her with that promise upon her lips.

When I saw her again, some time afterwards, she was more cheerful, yet I could plainly see it was the cheerfulness of resignation rather than of hope. What made her act so strangely? I asked her seriously, in an investigating spirit. But she could only tell me she *felt* so. I was perplexed and saddened by it. If she had shed a flood of tears now and then, while talking about the expected separation—like a woman, and naturally, I should have enjoyed such conversations as alluded to it, as a sweet luxury. As it was, I avoided them. I saw she could not help her sentiment, and I ceased to blame her, even in my heart; but it made me melancholy, and more than once my resolution was seriously shaken. I began in a general way to dread the approaching time of departure, and if it had been fixed three months later I am quite confident I should not have gone.

As the day came to be near at hand, however, my ambition and hopes were quickened, so much so that when the parting hour came, I bore myself like a man. She did not weep, even when I held her in my arms and impressed the last farewell kiss, but stood shrinkingly, with downcast eyes, saying—once only—in a tone like the dying tremor of a harp moved by the wind—"Good-by!" I knew that tone was from a soul wrung with deepest anguish, clouded with despair—my own soul told it me. But Europe was before me. The fondest hope of youthful imagination was to be gratified. Should I falter because of the superstitions of an over-loving heart? In this light I considered it, and walked boldly away.

It had been "in conclave decided" that my father and Joshua should accompany me as far as Philadelphia, hence the parting from home was not so painful as it would otherwise have been—to me; to those who remained there was no alleviation. They were all there, Delia and her family, too, standing at the old front gate, that morning when I returned from saying good-by to Fanny. The carriage was in readiness. They all knew where I had been, yet none alluded to it. They were all weeping, little Isaac, too, this time. Each embraced me fervently, saying, "God bless thee!" each in turn, and the painful ceremony was over. My father was in the carriage, sitting upright very firmly, and looking afar off while this was being done, taking apparently no note of surrounding circumstances, until I mounted to his side; then he coolly asked me if I was ready, and upon my replying in the affirmative, he uttered some severe sounds to the horses, which they obeyed promptly, and in a few minutes we were out of sight.

At the village we left the carriage, and taking the

public conveyance went on to Harrisburg. There we were joined by Joshua, and without delay proceeded on our journey towards Philadelphia. Our wayfaring experience was pretty much like others' on similar routes, being varied with partaking of mixed diet in a mixed company, and having our pockets divested of large coins for scant equivalents; and with two or three incidents such as a horse falling and breaking his leg, and a drunken driver falling off his box, and breaking the third commandment—pleasant variations when we could have no other, and helping to shorten the time, which was long enough, but at length came to an end with our entrance into the City of Friends—"of Brotherly Love," remarked Joshua; "so named in allusion to the early settlers, I suppose." It was Joshua's first pleasantry since we had set out, and it was quite refreshing. He had all the way been very solemn, discoursing, when he said anything, upon things which belong to the dark side of life.

Here I was to separate from the last landmarks of the old social field, and it came to pass with much poignant grief. Yet, as there was a general effort at self-restraint among us, the ceremony had something encouraging in it, and I passed away from their sight upon my distant journey, gathering fresh hopes every hour.

At New York I took passage on a merchantman, which set sail the next day after I went on board.

The first four-and-twenty hours were very pleasant, and I enjoyed myself so much, that I thought a life on the sea must be very desirable. My impressions, however, respecting sea life, were considerably changed on the third day, and continued changed. The slimy serpent, sea-sickness—the only genuine Sea Serpent—commenced its desolating ravages in my defenseless interior, and for four weeks and one day I was as one overthrown—mournfully cast down. Mighty Slough of Despond the Ocean was to me, indeed; yet I came out at last on the other side. Almost on all-fours—I needed half-a-dozen legs—I crawled upon the pier at Havre. "If such is Sea, I am content—albeit without content," I observed in the first assurance of solid footing, to a gentleman of glossy exterior, unmindful of the circumstance at the building of a certain tower. He smiled—because I did, I suppose, and executed an amazingly graceful bow, coming forward, and with several more faultless bows of different degrees of profundity, and not less than half-a-dozen score of false motions in half a score of seconds, communicated at once two things—his desire to render me infinite service, and my first impression of an actual, living Frenchman. I thanked him in the best French I could muster—which was not so very bad, as I had spent the leisure of more than a year instructing myself in the language—declining his services, and he retreated; but the impression remained—remains unto this day—to my mind, the whole French nation in small.

From Havre I proceeded directly to Paris. "Three months in Paris," I found written by Joshua in my pocket-memorandum. Accordingly I quartered myself deliberately, selecting the most eligible hotel and fixings, prudent regard of course being paid to my pecuniary resources.

I was not long in discovering that Paris was a large and thriving place—a great city; in fact, overgrown, too large to be comprehended even by the oldest inhabitant. Everything known in the known world, I had reason to believe, could be found there—from the lusty orang-outang down to a Franciscan monk, and from a French dandy the other way to an

American traveller—inclusive of all that they or their ancestors ever produced. It is true that during the three months I staid there, I never sought in vain for anything—except a letter from home. I was not idle in the pursuit of medical and pathological facts. Though necessarily desultory, I felt that my time was very profitably spent, and I had only to regret it was not three years, instead of three months, I could pass there. But I must go the round in one year, therefore I obeyed the directions which Joshua had inscribed, and went to Munich. There I remained six months, making very creditable progress. At Munich I received two letters—one from Cynthia and one from Fanny; full of love, both of them, yet how different! The same mysterious sentiment clung to Fanny, I could perceive, though she wrote in a strain of encouragement and hope. I answered them both elaborately, assuring Fanny, with a playful allusion to her unnatural solicitude, that I would soon be at home, and that I hoped she would join in the great laugh at her folly.

"Six months in Munich, three months in London, and then——a good long life at home," was the balance of Joshua's entry. I returned to Paris, intending from there to go to London. On the day of my arrival I fell in with an American, a medical student like myself. There was a similarity of temper and views, as well as ambition, which drew us together. We became, at once, warm friends. He had been some time in Paris, and was about starting for Berlin, and importuned me to accompany him, saying it would hinder me but a short time, and I would not lose by it. In an evil hour I consented to go with him.

The day before we left Paris, as I was walking along one of the principal business streets, somewhat heavy of heart, for I was not entirely satisfied with my promise,—perhaps a shadow from the future was upon me,—I was accosted by name. I did not at first recognize the voice, nor amongst the crowd see its source either—"Munn, Doctor Munn! Dang it all! you know me. Old friend Toom—Sam Toom," and out he came strongly individualized upon my vision:—out, and up to me, and took my hand in such an unreservedly friendly manner that I actually felt glad to see him, and told him so. "Away out in Paris here, such an eternal, watery distance from home. I'll be danged if it don't do my heart good"

—so much friendly feeling!—my heart warmed towards him every moment. I was about speaking. "I suppose," he interrupted "you'd like to hear from the old homestead, *and so forth*. I was there two months ago this day. Have you heard since?" He saw by the expression of my face—how quick he could read faces through his sleepy-looking eyes!—that I had not, and, hardly pausing, concluded, "They were all well, and spoke of you." He held my hand all this time, and I felt I was getting a new impression of his character. He knew it, I believe, and helped it on by saying rather abruptly—"Friend Ahasuerus, I am different from what I used to be. I have sown all my wild grain, deposited it deep in the earth. I've done all the mischief I'm going to do in this world. Henceforward a decent man must answer to the name Samuel Toom." I believed him. We talked of several interesting matters after that, standing there together an hour or more. He told me he was there with his employer on business. He inquired particularly about my intended movements, and on my expressing a reluctance towards going to Berlin, he urged me with considerable vehemence to go. At last our conversa tion came to an end, he asking me, at parting, if I wished to send anything home, as he was going directly there on his return to America.

He came to my lodgings that night, and I entrusted to him a brief communication directed to Joshua, informing him therein of my change of route, and of the probable delay it would occasion me,—stating, also, that I should not write again until I should reach London.

"You leave to-morrow, do you?" observed Samuel at the door, as he was going away—it was the third time he had made the observation since I had clearly informed him of my intention. "Yes," said I rather emphatically, for there was something in his countenance and manner that irritated me. I checked myself instantly, however, ashamed of my irritation, and was going to offer some parting remark in a modulated tone; but he was gone.

"Did you entrust to him anything valuable?" asked my friend, who had been present during the interview. I shook my head, asking in turn why he inquired. Instead of telling me the reason, he spoke of something else, and I thought no more *then* of the matter.

The next day we left for Berlin. At the first stopping-place I took up the morning paper to while away a few minutes during change of horses, and, as I ran over the local items, discovered the following:

"CASUALTY.—We learn that yesterday afternoon a young medical student, while assisting in dissection at —— Hospital, accidentally cut one of his fingers. Intense pain and swelling immediately ensued, which increased rapidly in spite of all the remedies used, and about ten o'clock he died in excruciating agonies. His name, as we understand, was Ahasuerus Munn, an American, in Paris to complete his studies."

"Singular coincidence of name and pursuit," I observed to my companion.

"Indeed, I think it is," he replied, and we laughed at it.

"Our journey was long, longer than I had anticipated, yet pleasant. The country we passed through is world-renowned, and between my friend and myself there was historic lore enough to give deep interest to much that we saw.

In Berlin I found so much to give me pleasure and intellectual profit, that instead of two months—the time I had prospectively allowed for my sojourn—nearly three were gone before I was ready to depart.

Thus far fortune had smiled. Thus far my future

had grown brighter and brighter—how benign! how inspiring! Now it was suddenly darkened. On the eve of departure from Berlin I was taken very ill. For several weeks my life was despaired of. During this illness my new friend showed by his conduct, that I had not been deceived in him. Through his unwearied attentions—and measurably through his skill, I was rescued from the grave.

One day, during my convalescence, a German gazette was brought to me that I might amuse myself in reading. Almost the first paragraph I read, contained the startling intelligence that the United States of America had declared war against Great Britain. The Last War, you understand. It was bitter intelligence to me. Had I gone to London, as Joshua had directed, I might then have been on my way home under safe conduct. Now I had a desperate gauntlet to run. If unsuccessful——O, my God! I could not bear the dreadful thought. There was something more than hope deferred that made the conjecture so hideous. A vague suspicion was in my mind—too vague, if not too dreadful, for utterance.

As soon as I was able to travel, I was impatient to be on my way home. My friend consented to accompany me as far as Paris, and together we thitherward directed our course. We arrived at that city in safety, where I parted, with deep regret, from my companion, and went immediately to Havre. I there found an American vessel—an armed brig—lying in port for refit. She was to sail in a few days for New York, and with gratitude to Heaven, and renewed hope, I took passage in her. Though stimulated for a time with the incident of finding an American vessel without delay, that was going directly home, a strange uneasiness began to haunt me—deepening into melancholy. It was a great distance. The ocean swarmed with hostile fleets. I *could* not be delayed—yet I might be. There was a multitude of adverse chances. My depression and anxiety were agonizing.

Our voyage was pleasant—*very* pleasant—for many days. We were almost home. The load was lightening.

One evening—according to reckoning, we were five days fair sailing from New York—as the sun went down, a large vessel under full sail, appeared upon the western horizon. Hitherto we had encounterd friends only, and therefore the stranger, though contemplated with distrust, did not beget much anxiety

Before dark, it was announced by the commander that the stranger was making a tack, and that her course lay directly towards us. Early in the evening the wind ceased, and we were all night becalmed. Sufficient anxiety remained in my mind to call me at break of day on deck, where I found considerable excitement prevailing. The wind had sprung up again towards morning, and every sail was set.

"What is the trouble?" I asked of the first mate, who was passing hurriedly, with a drawn sword in his hand. He answered by pointing astern out upon the sea. I looked, and to my deep dismay saw, not more than a mile distant, a huge man of war, bearing directly down upon us.

I will not detail to you what happened—only saying that on our part it was a hopeless race. In less than two hours we were overtaken, and after a short and terrific struggle were boarded. In my despair I fought—fought like a madman. With the death of nearly three-fourths of our company, the sanguine deed was accomplished—the brig was taken, and those of us who had been secured alive, were thrust into the hold of the victor.

We were taken to Barbadoes. On the way I was

not without hope; but when we arrived there, and I was cast into a deep dungeon, and the massive door, which mocked at the idea of escape, was closed and bolted upon me, I sank to the cold, stone floor, longing for immediate death—so hopeless.

It may seem strange that I was in such utter despair. It is true that to be imprisoned, and that, too, far from the ministrations of loving ones, was dreadful, but I knew the war could not long continue, not many years at most, and when that should end, I would be free—perhaps before. Yet these I did not think of. I wanted freedom then, then—or never! The dark suspicion to which I have before alluded, had deepened, within the last few days, into belief. Samuel had dealt treacherously by me—would deal treacherously to the sacrifice of my long-cherished, most precious hopes. How clearly I saw it! How bitterly did I curse myself! Infatuated wretch! stupidly blind! Except the short letter I had entrusted to him, I had not written home since leaving Munich. That letter would not be delivered—ay, I knew it. Why did I not return to Paris, after reading that local item—question the editor—know it was not villainy—before I went on. Stupid fool! laughing at it as a joke!—laughing at the dagger which was to enter my heart! I saw, or thought I saw, the rash, yet fiendish machination, in all its subtlety. It drove me deeper into despair—if such could be—the more I reflected upon it. My body gave way under the mental torture. A raging fever consumed me, and wildness was in my brain. They took me to the hospital. How they saved me I cannot conceive. My constitution had been already shattered, and I had a fixed determination to die—I demanded death.

When I was again able to walk, I was taken back to the dungeon. Happily for me, though I did not so consider it then, I was furnished with a comfortable room, and was decently fed.

In the exhaustion of strength, I seemed to have less capacity for misery, and for a while experienced a sort of negative enjoyment. As comparative health returned, a deep melancholy, that had something of resignation in it, took possession of me.

Slow months passed. I was as one in a dream. I lived only in the present. The future—a blackness from which hope shrank; the past—in sleep it came to me, as a nun might visit the haunts of early life. Only in sleep could I bear it.

Could they but know that I still lived—that I would some day come to their loving embrace. They could not know. They believed me dead. They had reason so to believe. That reason might not have existed. Bitter consciousness! I could but curse myself. I have said I lived only in the present. There were shadows from the past—such shadows!—came to me when I was *not* asleep. They came when hope would persuade me, and cast their mantle over my soul. "Samuel is unhappy." "I know he has been bad to *thee*." Did that tender heart know what it revealed in these? Had I known, I would have told her. But I only know they were grating sounds. Now, in my agony, they were as shafts of burning light.

Sometimes I listened to the whisperings of Hope, when she told me all these dark fears were empty shadows—that the heart which had throbbed against my own, in the sweet ecstasy of requited love, still beat true to me—that the fiend would not prevail. When I so listened I was happy—yea, happy.

Yet it was all a dream—wild and dark—with these few gleams of light, like falling stars.

The second autumn of my imprisonment was

gently laying waste the earth, when one day a sealed note was put into my hand. I eagerly tore it open. It was my passport. I was free! I troubled not myself to know how I came by my release. I was free. That was enough. Free to go—where? Home. I trembled—not with joy. "Home" was no longer a word of enchantment. It conjured evil. I dreaded to go, yet could not stay. The wild, dark dream continued.

On the wide sea, beneath a kindly sun, and fanned by vivifying breezes, hope revived within me. When the shores of my native land opened mistily to my vision, and the sound of glad voices from hearts hoping without reserve filled the air about me, I hoped with them, yet not without reserve, alas!

We landed at New York. Without delay I went on to Philadelphia—thence to Harrisburg. I came to the last-named place early one evening, and being fatigued with rapid journeying, I put up for the night —at the old hotel, which had been like a second home to me. It had changed hands, as I saw immediately on my entrance.

"Does Doctor Noyles stay here?" I asked—with what eagerness you may imagine—of the clerk.

"Am not acquainted with the gentleman, sir. I think no such name is on the list, sir."

He looked. While he was looking, a middle-aged man, well dressed, and of easy bearing, accosted me.

"Are you acquainted with Doctor Noyles?" he said.

"I was, years ago," I replied.

"So was I, many years ago."

"Have you seen him lately?" I inquired, hoping through him, perhaps, to learn Joshua's place of stopping, as the clerk had just denied the presence of his name upon the list.

"About two years ago I saw him last—an hour or so—at Richmond, Virginia. His health was not good, and he was suffering under some bereavement, that made him very melancholy."

"Did he tell you the name of the friend he had lost?" I asked, tears starting in my eyes—the haunting conjecture that I had believed and disbelieved, fought against and shrunk before so long, must it yet be true? My brain swam with the fierce tumult of the instant.

"He *did* tell me the name," said he, after a short effort at recollection; "but for the life of me I can't recall it now. A young man who had studied with him. Singular I can't think of the name. Aha! useless. Died in Europe. Accidental death. He seemed to mourn very much, and was travelling in part to divert his mind."

It was true! I *had* seen the rash machination in all its subtlety. Oh, the agony of that moment! I trembled, my breath was short, and my heart labored as in an overwhelming flood!

"You are not well," remarked the gentleman, looking upon me with surprise and anxiety.

Fearful struggle! Yet but a moment! I replied with a calmness that astonished me—"What you have said interests me very much. That young man's name was Munn."

"Well, yes, I think it was. Munn? Munn? Yes, it was."

"And I am he!"

"Indeed! False report, then. I'm glad of it—I am so. It will do the old man's heart good. He has had trouble in his day—scathing, corroding affliction—worse than death by fagot Oh, such days!—awful days! My young friend, we must go and visit the Doctor together, to-morrow. With one or two brief exceptions, it is now more than twenty-five years since we have sat and wandered together in friendly intercourse, and I have come nearly five hundred miles in these troublous times on purpose to see him, and renew, for a while, at leisure, the broken thread —broken—ah! I will not think of it.

In the morning the acquaintance of the previous evening joined me after breakfast, and we went down the street so familiar—familiar though changed—towards the old office. When we came to the door, I knocked. No answer. I was about to knock again, when I noticed to my great surprise that the old sign was gone, and a new one, with a strange name, occupied its place. He has retired from business, was my first thought. We should not find him in the city. No place more likely at which to meet him, than my father's house. I expressed these to my companion, and he promptly agreed to accompany me home. The stage would not go out till after dinner, I knew; and to pass the time, I proposed a walk about the city.

It was a pleasant stroll, though to me melancholy. The darkness of my future—it had never been so dark before—contrasted with the distant, beaming past, which every step brought up, weighed upon me, yet it was like the sway of mournful music, that peoples the realm of oblivion. We were returning. The old grave-yard was at our right hand. As we came along to the gate, my companion stopped, tried it, found it unfastened, and as by common impulse, we walked in.

"This place is not new to me, my friend," remarked my companion, as he closed the gate, "nor do I come here from idle curiosity. I did not want to come to this sacred spot until I had seen Joshua, that——but I could not resist. Will you bear with my caprice and amuse yourself for a short time while I go to yonder corner?"

His voice was thick with emotion, and as he looked at me for my assent, I saw tears in his eyes.

I cheerfully complied with his request, and he went away towards the corner. Interested in his movements, I looked after him. He drew near the corner. Suddenly he stopped, lifting both hands as if in amazement. Then he turned and beckoned to me. I hurriedly obeyed his signal, and as I approached, saw that he was standing by a new-made grave, leaning on the marble slab at its head, and convulsed with weeping. What! Oh, it could not be—it must not be. "Died," thus I read from the cold stone, my heart and breath stilled with the heavy wave of anguish that is like death—"on the 17th of July, 1814, Joshua Noyles, aged fifty-five years and three months."

As a lurid flash it was, and then came darkness—blindness. Every faculty, every sense was benumbed. I should have sunk to the ground but for my companion's timely assistance.

It was several minutes before I recovered. When I did, my friend had ceased weeping, and holding my hand, he talked to me—told me there, as we sat together upon the hallowed earth, what in happier days I had so wished to know. Briefly he uttered it. "My young friend, let us rejoice that he is gone. They are now together. You see another grave here, close by the side of this one. In that lie the remains of my only sister—once so full of life and hope. She was beautiful—a frail, spiritually beautiful creature, and to her natural gifts was added all that wealth could bestow. Joshua loved her--worshiped her. His youthful soul, noble above ten thousand, adored her as its high angel. There was a young, proud woman lived in the same town—Toom was the man she afterwards married. She is dead, now, I think. This woman loved Joshua, and sought to win him. In every attempt she failed, and then in a despair she sought revenge. Joshua and my sister were to be married. She contrived and executed a plot, dark and malicious almost beyond belief. She managed to persuade my sister that Joshua was false; she even went so far as to demonstrate by means of forged letters that he had pledged himself to *her*, and had sealed the pledge with a criminal act. I was young then—a sailor, too, in distant seas. Had I been at home, it would have gone differently with them all, perhaps. My sister treated Joshua with scorn. The noble youth sought an explanation, but no opportunity was given. He left the place, and went—no one knew where. For two years he wandered. What must those years not have been to him! In the meantime I returned. I learnt the facts. I knew Joshua, ay, too well not to know that he was innocent. I showed my sister that she had been deceived. She saw it plainly, and unspeakable anguish harrowed her night and day. Her health forsook her. Pulmonary consumption, to which she was predisposed, took fatal hold. She was near the grave when Joshua returned—ghastly shadow of his former self. They were reconciled. But the sun had set, and there would be no more day. In a few weeks my sister died—in Joshua's arms, and he told her before she ceased to hear, just as she was passing from earth, that in heaven she should be his wife.

For many months I was with him night and day. It seems to me no mortal could be more wretched than he was, and live. I used often to beg him to cease his wild lamentations, they so probed me from mere sympathy. Time wore it away, however, and before I left him, he could speak almost with calmness of the awful event. They are together, now, in heaven."

The stage was ready, and shaking hands with my new friend—he had now no need to go with me—I was soon on my way home—home, as one borne on a subterranean stream. I came to the village in the night, and walked on towards the old mansion. As I drew near, the wind moaned through the old forest—a voice!

I will not tell you, I cannot tell you, how they received me. A wild tumult of joy it was, almost too much for them to bear. But at length they grew calm; and then we talked together. How did they get report of my death? I knew, but yet I asked. Samuel had shown it them in a French gazette. What was his object—or had he any? A dismal, fleeting hope that he had had none, prompted my inquiry. He had an object. They had never seen it before, and now thought it a rash, fool-hardy scheme of his. "Yet," said my father, "he knew the political state of the country. He knew war was inevitable. It was a desperate chance, and he adopted it desperately, with hope that in the dangers of crossing the ocean, thee might fall a victim; or, hoping if thee came, to accomplish his purpose before. He had nothing to lose, and everything to gain."

How came my father to know so much about the scheme and its object? Something had publicly come to pass. What was it? The question was in my heart, but I gave it not voice. I could not.

The next day, as I sat in Cynthia's room, looking towards Mr. Cline's—I had been talking of my adventures—Cynthia began to weep. I divined the cause. "Tell me," said I, passionately, "dear sister, tell me. Do not reserve it. I must know the truth."

"Oh, my brother!" she exclaimed, "forgive her. she clung long to thee, even after she fully believed thee dead. Samuel was good. He attended divine worship. He joined the society. Everybody thought he was going to be a better man. The Clines thought so more than any, and they encouraged him. He was here several months. At last he asked her to be his wife. She refused. He importuned. He begged me to intercede for him. Forgive me, Ahasuerus; I told her to marry him. She still refused. Her parents insisted. When she promised to marry him, I was by. I never heard such eloquence as Samuel's then. She told him she would be his wife, but he must wait till the next spring. When she told him this, he turned as pale as death, but said nothing. He went away to Boston, or somewhere. In the spring he came back, and they were married. They are now living in Boston. His health is very poor, and they say he drinks. He was only shamming. Mr. Cline's folks know it now. Pity her, Ahasuerus, and forgive her. It would kill her to know that thou still livest."

Thus my hope was smitten out of me, crushed, and buried——for ever?

Several months passed gloomily on. I had no ambition to begin the practice of my profession, and delayed it, staying around the home of my childhood, wrapped in a melancholy abstraction, which my friends labored in vain to dissipate.

One day—I had been at home seven or eight months—my father came from the village in an unusually blithesome mood. I met him at the door, and he shook hands with me, though he had not been gone more than two hours. I was astonished; and still more so, when he put a newspaper in my hands, pointing, with a smile, to a paragraph headed, "DIED." The next instant I saw the cause of his feelings. In connection, I read, "Suddenly, on the 9th inst., at his residence in —— St., Samuel Toom. (Pennsylvania papers please copy.)" The paper had come from Fanny; her own dear hand-writing was on the margin, and on the wrapper.

A star was in the sky—a morning star. The long, dark night was at an end; a new day was coming to my weary soul.

The brother went immediately to Boston. In a few weeks he returned, bringing Fanny with him.

After a decent interval, I visited her. She was not

much changed, only that she looked more sad than when I had last seen her. Our first interview was short and formal. The next was longer, and so the next. Then all restraint was taken off. We wept in each other's arms, and were lovers again.

A few happy months, and the union of souls, so long known in heaven, was consecrated before men, with great rejoicing; for every one round about knew the history of our love, and gloriously exulted in the bliss which had at last come to us.

Gentlemen, this is the end of the special train of facts. You must make your own peroration, for it's late, I'm sure, and I must go to bed.

"In view of the special facts, then,—the train thereof, I should say,—and the importuning of *a* fact, I pronounce this meeting actually in a state of adjournment, *si—ne ——die.*"

Thus remarked the lawyer, with labored articulation, in the midst of a most distorting stretch; and we all arose quietly, and quietly went our several ways, ending in bed.

The following Sunday—and it was the next day but one—I stayed at a farm-house. The family all went away to church, and left me alone. As I had the other two stories sketched down, it occurred to me, that perhaps some day I, or some one else, might be found in want of amusement; and, taking somehow a special interest in this story—long as it was—I thought I would add it to the others, thus making, at least, a pleasant reminiscence, which I could bring forth on a future occasion, if not for the gratification of some one else, at any rate for my own. So I spent the day in jotting down the leading points of the Quaker's narration, in the evening consigning all to my old portmanteau for safe keeping, where, in a forgotten corner, they remained until the commencement of the present occasion.

CHAPTER VIII.

(Of course I did not tell my story. Yet I had one in my head, and would have told it had opportunity been given. I introduce it here, under the general impression that the series would be incomplete without it. It is not a story from my own experience, but a slightly modified one which I remember of hearing when I was a boy. An old man, who used sometimes to come to our house, told it once to my parents and myself, on a quiet summer evening, for our entertainment. He told it with a great deal of feeling, and it affected me—a child—very much. That it will have a corresponding effect upon "children of larger growth," for whom it is now intended, is, on my part, only to be hoped.

With this parenthetical preface, I proceed, giving a title according to my fancy, and adopting the manner in which the old man told the story—as nearly as I can remember.)

ELLEN'S GRAVE.

A little less than two years ago, I visited my native town. Thirty years had gone by in the interval since my leaving it, and I found, naturally, that great changes had taken place in everything almost, and in nothing more than in the old church-yard. As the town had become populated, so had that, gathering its denizens in proportion. Aristocratic obelisks and iron railings; heavy marble slabs, with angel figures and drooping trees elaborately wrought upon them; small slabs, with cherub figures and drooping buds; unhewn slabs of common stone, with no device—without a name! Many, very many, of these were new to me. Many of the names, too, were new; yet some were old—familiar as household words, and as dear.

It was a sunny Sabbath afternoon, in early autumn, that I first went, after my arrival in the town, to visit the old grave-yard. I was in a melancholy mood, or I should not have gone, for I deem the resting-place of the dead too sacred a spot to be approached, except the soul be pre-attuned to the solemn strain whose echo is ever there; and as I wandered, reading the names which in years long gone I had so often heard, I grew more melancholy, for now and then a life-history—what else than a history of sorrows?—flashed from afar upon my quickened memory. Here a brave man, stalwart and sublime, who had fought for and reared a precious growth of innocence, and worth, and beauty, to see it fade in its ripeness and in its bloom—passing from his frantic grasp, yet beckoning to him—had lain him down, that he might go and be with the treasure he had lost. Here a meek woman, a widow—many years a widow—had gone to rest; rest which she could not find on earth, for she was the mother of an ungrateful son. Here a child, an orphan boy, had finished his earthly course. He was a child of promise, and in his death there was no common sorrow, for as everybody knew his history, so everybody loved him.

Thus I went on, enjoying with a kind of mournful surprise what the familiar names brought up. With mournful surprise. There was one I had in reserve. —It could not surprise me. No; I knew, ay, well, where it was, and I reserved it to the last. When at length I came to it, lingeringly, fascinated, yet stung with anguish, I removed my hat, and leaning upon my cane, I read (though I had no need), the inscription. "In memory," so it ran "of Ellen Lucas, who died March 7th, 17—, aged 19 years, one month and three days." As I read, I wept. It was but a gush, as the last scene, heavy and dim, was before me: — the gathered friends, the flickering lights, the sobs, the broken wails, the marble figure, and a smile which the spirit just departed had left to tell us whither it had gone. It was but a gush, for that smile carried me back to her childhood. I remembered her as she was when I first saw her, a prattling little creature, her words yet burdened with the charming lisp of infancy. Bright blue eyes she had—how bright!—and lips that might have kissed an angel's, yet defiled them not, and around those lips and bright eyes often played a strangely vivid smile—so thrillingly beautiful, that to tempt it forth was a feast at which the heart was never sated, and which could never be forgotten.

I was a young man then, studying law; and as I went to and from my place of study, I used often to stop and watch little Ellen playing in the yard before her mother's house. So often I did this, that she came to know me well, and would come, when I asked her, to the fence and kiss me. One day as I came along, she was sitting on the step at the gate, crying. Touched with sympathy, I took her up gently and asked the cause of her grief.

"I called them, and they would not come," she answered regretfully, and choked with sobs.

"Who would not come?" I inquired.

"The pretty birds," was her reply. I questioned her further, and she showed me on the grass a little blanket with some crumbs of bread upon it. This she had prepared for some birds that had been singing on a neighboring tree. She had called them, and they would not come, but singing awhile, had flown away. "Why did they not come?" I asked with no certain object. She did not reply directly, but said in a tone wonderfully pathetic for a child, "I love them, but they don't love me."

I wiped away her tears, soothing her, and presently she forgot her disappointment and its cause. Not so with me.

Little Ellen was the daughter of a widow—her father she had never seen. She had a brother three years older than herself—an only brother, and she an only sister. He was a bold, healthful lad, with strongly-marked features, and a fierce energy that seemed almost too great for one so young.

A year or two later, when they began to go to school together, I remember how they used to appear on their way hand in hand—she looking at him, at the trees, at the birds, and flashing her strangely beautiful smile into the faces of passers by—he with his jacket thrown open, his cap almost off his head, his long hair tossed by the wind, looking fierce, unutterable things into the great future which was ever opening upon his gleaming sight. A noble boy —such as one points out proudly to a friend.

I had not ceased my tarryings now and then to watch little Ellen in her sports. One day, as I was passing, her brother was with her in the front yard playing. He was trimming a kite, she building a play-house. I stopped, and stood looking, unobserved by them. Suddenly she turned from her play-house, as though she had lost all interest in it for ever, and asked her brother what he was going to be when he should have grown up.

"I don't know," he replied, engaged with his kite, then in a moment, recollecting himself, continued, gazing off into the sky, his face beaming as though he saw some glorious object—"Yes I do, too. I'm going to be a great man. I'm going to be rich, and have a gold watch, and have all the money I want to give to beggars. And I'll make a silk kite, and have a cord ten-thousand-thousand feet long, so I can fly it away up above the clouds where the eagles went last fall."

"Wouldn't you ever want to get married?" she asked with timid earnestness.

"No," said he stoutly. "I'd have you live with me. We shouldn't have to go to school then, and we could do just as we please. I'd like to see Ben Bottles snow-ball me then, and say he'd tell my mother if I touched him!"

"I'm going to get married when I grow up," said the little girl after a minute's pause—"I'm going to marry a prince and be a queen, and have glass dolls as big as I am, and gold play-houses, and a great room, as big as our parlor, full of flowers, and——everything."

The brother seemed not to have heard it, for he took his kite, and with a loud hurrah started towards the common. She turned around, looked with a sor rowful dissatisfaction upon her unfinished play-house, and walked slowly into the house.

Thus Ellen's childhood came beamingly to my mind as I stood by her sunken grave, and it dried my tears.

Over a lapse of several years—years of absence from my native town—my mind leapt, and I saw her in the first ripeness of womanhood—the child developed and intensified—still looking upon the world as a garden with flowers springing up everywhere. She was beautiful in the world's estimation—very beautiful, and as witty as beautiful. The proud, whether of riches mental or material, sought her society, and flatterers were ever humming honeyed words in her ear.

I renewed her acquaintance—not to sip and flatter as others did, but that I might be her friend and guard her; for I knew how narrow was the pathway which she was treading with such airy tread, and the depth of the gulfs which yawned on either side. It was a pleasant duty, and when I told her I had taken it upon me, she thanked me for it, and with the deep earnestness for which she was peculiar, confessed her need of a firm, sagacious friend, who would always tell her the truth and love her for her virtues. I should not perhaps have volunteered to sustain this relation to her had her brother been at home. He was at college—away, pursuing the objects of his high ambition, and scarcely knowing more of her than that she was his sister, and that he loved her.

As I became more intimately acquainted with her, I noticed a strange trait. I was long making the discovery complete, for she kept it hid in her inmost heart. In her childhood I had seen it, but had deemed it then only an idle fancy, and now hoped it might prove nothing else. From the reading she indulged in I first surmised it, and then from remarks dropped in careless as well as in earnest moods. I at last came to know the fact. It was this: An unbounded admiration of rank. The tinsel and the courtly sound of rank so fascinated her, though she knew them only in imagination, that the land of her birth was to her an object of contempt because it did not cherish them. Strange trait, indeed; yet oftener felt than seen, I wis. When I sought to dispossess her of it, it was hidden deeper from me and disowned, and I relinquished the attempt.

One day, several months after my return, a stranger came to our town, and took lodgings in the same hotel at which I was staying. The fact was not notable, but the habits and appearance of the individual were somewhat so. He was apparently between twenty-five and thirty years of age. His dress was of the latest cut, and punctiliously adjusted. Upon his upper lip flourished a heavy, glossy growth of beard, exquisitely arranged. His hair was long and curling, and was combed smoothly behind his ears. He wore gold-mounted spectacles, with side-glasses, completely hiding the expression of his eyes, and carried a golden-headed cane. Among the folds of his shirt-bosom, gleamed an ornament of strange device —a golden heart, intricately wound with exceedingly fine golden wire, and pierced with a diamond-pointed dart. Except this he wore no jewelry.

For nearly two weeks after his arrival, he was not seen below stairs. He took his meals in his room, and received no company. One afternoon, as I was standing at the door of the hotel, watching the people passing to and fro on their divers errands of good or evil, I felt a gentle touch upon my shoulder, and, turning round, I saw the stranger before me. With the exquisite modulation of a native Frenchman, he addressed me in that tongue, soliciting me to share with him the unutterable pleasure of a short promenade. Assuming the best grace and the best French I could, I informed him I was at leisure, and should be happy in attending him. He placed his arm in mine, and we walked on together.

"You are, as well as myself, from foreign parts," he began, still addressing me in French. I informed him that I was an American, rather testily, I fear, for I thought he was inexcusably dull, or was making game of me; and I informed him, moreover, that my knowledge of the French language was very imperfect, and requested him, if he could as well speak English, to do so. Upon this he craved my pardon, and with an accent as perfect as had been his French, he proceeded in English. "I was laboring under a mistake, my dear sir. I was sure you were French-born. Can it be I have been so mistaken? You will surely pardon me."

This left me in so awkward a predicament that I kept silence, and we walked on a number of minutes, neither of us speaking. At last, becoming somewhat annoyed with the taciturnity of my companion, I turned towards him, thinking to address some casual remark to him, when I was startled with the steady, piercing look which I met. The sensation of being in the vicinity of a huge, wrathful viper, took such deep hold upon me that a slight shudder shot along my nerves.

"By the way," said he quickly, yet carelessly, "have you been long in this delightful town?"

This is my birth-place," I replied, "but I have been absent from it many years, having returned only a few months since."

"Aha! Your birth-place? and you have been absent many years? It must be pleasant to return from distant wanderings to your birth-place, to meet your old companions; to kiss sweet lips that were at the mother's breast when you went away; and to waltz with those who then knew nothing of passion's glow; to read in the cool, steady eye of the matron, the tale of passion, ripe then, now plucked, enjoyed, and existing only in memory. Indeed it must be pleasant;—or am I on forbidden ground? Perhaps you are married?"

"No," I replied, telling the truth. The next moment I continued, with a wink, "I prefer single life; it gives greater latitude, you know."

He saw the object of my remark, perhaps, and only responded with a smile. We walked in silence again. Suddenly he spoke in an altered tone.

"I am a wanderer. The world is my home—my inheritance the future. Time is my father. All will be his, then why not mine? I like ruins. I take after my father. But Pleasure is my mother, and pleasure goes before ruins; otherwise life would be a cart-before-the-horse sort of an affair, and we would do better to die first and live afterwards—not having the fear of death before our eyes, eh? Isn't that good philosophy?"

I bowed assent.

"Would you think I ever had any trouble?" he continued, resuming his gay tone. "Yet a veil must hide something. Do you understand that? I have lost much, may gain much. Aha! may gain a great deal, and lose it afterwards. So goes the world. But the Devil take the odds! The future is my inheritance. Beauty is all around me. I can enjoy *that—as a man of principle*, you know. What is man without principle in this world? Do you know what I heard a dying man say once? Said he, 'I would give all the *principal* I possess for one more hour of life.' I thought at first it was a blasphemy, and was going to be horrified, when a friend whispered in my ear, 'his avarice is melting.' 'Yes, and give heed to the value of money,' I responded, seeing the point. That offer was about equal to the actual performance of a fellow of my acquaintance, who, in a fit of jealousy, determined to shoot his rival. He was very rich, and that the justice of the deed might stick out, he bartered his possessions for a bank note, and making a wad of it, heaped the favor, with the addition of a little lead, upon said rival, killing, of course, two birds at once—three in fact, for they hung him, notwithstanding his generosity, or rather because of its being misdirected. You understand, there was no object in defending him. I tell you, you must have money, if you wish to appear in a favorable light before a jury." The last sentence was spoken in a low, emphatic tone, as though it contained valuable information.

Our walk was finished, and we re-entered the hotel. "Will you go up to my apartment?" he asked, albeit releasing his arm from mine. I did as he wanted me to—politely declined, and we separated.

I felt relieved when he was gone; yet there was something in the recollection of his manner that drew me towards him, and I would fain excuse his lightness of bearing, his appearance of hollowness. There was an undefined impression clung to me that he had seen great trouble, and that "that veil *did* hide something," and in spite of the viperine look that had so startled me, I felt quite warm at heart towards him as I dwelt upon the recollection of his general manner. I wanted to see him again. This want was soon gratified. The fourth day after our walk, I received a note inviting me very politely to come to his room. I went. He met me with great urbanity of demeanor, leading me to a chair, overwhelming me with solicitous remarks concerning my health and prospects. When he had done with my health and prospects, he fell to talking of his own, concluding. "I'm very lonely, too, here in this little out-of-the-way town—I beg your pardon, sir, but it isn't a city, you know, and I have been accustomed to the excitement of balls, and plays, and lectures, and all that sort of thing, you know, and I must have a substitute, or I shall absolutely perish."

There was much earnestness in his manner, so much that my sympathy was considerably excited, and I told him I would do all that within me lay to afford him social pastime. He expressed much gratitude for my promise, and to convince him of my sincerity, I invited him to accompany me to a select party which was to meet at Mrs. Lucas's that evening. He accepted my invitation, and we went. On the way he gave me a card, upon which I saw elegantly penned, "Leopold, Paris." "You will please to introduce me accordingly," he said.

In the faultless elegance and soft fascination of M. Leopold that evening, I saw nothing of the wayward uncertainty which he had manifested to me when alone with him. There seemed to be but one feeling in the company towards him—that of admiration and respect. Though the oldest there, so completely did I yield to his influence, that I could have embraced him in the ardor of strongest friendship. Could Ellen remain indifferent? Her feelings were quite too evident. Hours after, when the social ravishment had wasted itself in sweet dreams, I awoke in the calm night, and reflected upon it. I was conscience-stricken. A still, small voice stabbed me with its murmuring "All is not well." But I hooded the tormenter, saying, "If bad come out of it, I shall have done my duty. If there be danger, my warning will avert it." Did I understand the female heart? What virtuous bachelor ever did?

From that time forward, M. Leopold seemed to shun me. Why? Had he only wished to *use* me? Deep as it cut, I could not help the inference. When I became fully aware that he really did shun me, I repented deeply the act I had done, and with vision sharpened by the injury my pride had sustained, and anxiety concerning my lovely *protégé* I watched his movements closely. I found no alleviation in watching, for I saw too plainly that Ellen had attracted him, and, though the warning had been given and repeated, I saw that he was taking strong hold upon her heart. It did not matter now to say I had striven to avert the danger. My conscience smote me sorely that I had brought them together. Danger. Is there danger? I sometimes asked my judgment. He is a villain, my judgment told me, and I believed it. Perhaps he would deal honorably with her. In that hope there was comfort, and I did not resist it. Perhaps, too, prejudice warped my judgment. I had only my first impression of him, and the fact of his shunning me, from which to infer. In the former I might be mistaken, in the latter my feelings were necessarily concerned. Yet that would not do. Thirty-five years of varied experience in human nature did not tend to promote charity in such a case. Still he might deal honorably by her, and upon this I rested—uneasily.

Of course, as M. Leopold had come forth into society, the whole town had run wild after him. He had become, at once, the talk and the thought of all, and continued so. How could it be otherwise? A foreigner, with a courtier-like name, young, handsome, brilliant, fascinating, circulating among a fashion-loving, yet comparatively unsophisticated people. When I saw how great was his popularity, I wished much that I could think of him only as I had seen him that first evening, at Mrs. Lucas's. But I could not.

He still continued to shun me. Why? Did he wish to make Ellen his wife, what could be his object in thus treating her chosen friend? If not—ay, then he might have an object. I had not thought of it so, before; yet I would not, when the idea flashed into my mind, allow it to take form. I was powerless for good, and must now abide the result as it might be. I found means at last to quiet my conscience, but my forebodings—foolish as I tried to consider them, sometimes—would not depart.

M. Leopold was often at Mrs. Lucas's, and occasionally I met him there. I could not help but admire him, though towards me he was so refinedly civil—

so exquisitely icy. What could Ellen do but love him? And when I looked upon him, I had it not in my heart to dissuade her, if to dissuade her had been possible. Yet there were moments when I was alone and calm, in which I would have made any sacrifice, ther than of life, to have induced her to banish him from her presence. Thus my mind wavered, with no tangible cause. The vacillation made me timorous, which was, perhaps, the chief reason why I did not, the third time, sound my warning in Ellen's ears.

M. Leopold's attentions to Ellen, and their analogically-established marriage, became the talk of the excited town, and except where envy was plainly at work, no objection was urged. All believed in a sunny result. Had anybody else such first impressions as I had? Evidently not.

Walking in the street one day, I was most agreeably surprised at meeting, in company with a friend who introduced him to me, Morgan Lucas, Ellen's brother. I had known him well when he was a boy, but had not seen him since. Time had done much for him. Large, yet gracefully symmetrical in form, he stood before me in the noble bearing of fully developed manhood. The same fierce, dark eye, now illumined with the meaning fire of high-toned intelli gence, and steadied with the experience of profitably spent years. He had just returned from college, and was, so he said, now prepared to enter upon the duties of life. Alas! that the first duty was to be so severe. But a wise Ruler had decreed it.

The next day he called at my office. I was alone when he came. After the first gush of friendly greeting, I saw that a shade rested upon his countenance.

"Have you seen Ellen, lately?" said he, with a tone of voice in which anger, sadness, and tenderness were strangely blended.

"Last week," I replied; "why do you ask?"

"Do you know that fellow who styles himself Leopold, who is hanging about town here, doing nothing? He boards at the same hotel with you, I believe."

"I know him, yes; but I know nothing about him," I answered, far more deeply interested than I wanted to appear.

"Well, he's a scamp—take my word for it."

"Have you seen him?" I inquired.

"He came to our house last night. He's a talented rogue, though. He made an excellent show. But I could read him. Oh! I hate that cobra-de-capella look of his."

Our first impressions, then, agreed; but I did not

betray my feelings, only remarking, "I am sorry he does not please you, for it is said he is to be your brother."

I had gone too far. He put his hand upon my shoulder, and looking into my face with a keen, earnest glance, as though he would read my soul, said—"Do you remember Ellen and me when we were thoughtless children? Do you remember how I loved her then? Do you know that that love has grown with my growth, centering all my love for the sex in her, until my very life would seem to depend upon hers? I know you were a friend to us children, and I believe you are our friend now. If you are, do not mock me so with words. If I ever needed the judicious support of an experienced friend, I do now. Mr. D——, I believe that Leopold to be a scoundrel, and that he does not intend to marry Ellen, but to ruin her—if—Oh, my God! Don't let me think it!"

The veil I had assumed was gone. "Morgan," said I, grasping his hand, "I *am* your friend, and you may open your heart to me. Now tell me why you think he is a villain."

"Well, I will," he replied. "This morning I was talking with Ellen about him. With the utmost sin cerity she told me he was a prince in disguise. 'Prince of blacklegs,' said I. 'Oh, don't talk so, brother,' said she, with that deep tone of injured love which you know she might have on such an occasion, and forthwith brought me a letter which purported to be from a distinguished man in France, written in English, mind you. In that letter he was addressed as 'His Most Serene Highness,' and lots of other such nonsense. I asked her to let me see some of his handwriting, which she did with that open confidence I so love in her, dear girl! I compared the writing carefully, and there it was, as plain as day, the same. Now, you know her weakness, and don't you suppose he knows it? And do you suppose he would have played that trick off upon her, if he only wished to marry her like an honest man? Strange that she don't see it! I told her so; but she began to cry, and that was the last of it, then, of course. Oh! I hope it is not too late."

I knew not what to say. Here my worst apprehensions were taking the form of reality. I arose and walked the floor of my office, thinking of what I should advise. I could think of no better course than to wait and watch. "We can do nothing except as we may persuade her," I said at last. "Perhaps what you said this morning may have an effect." I talked on for some time in this strain, and then he left me, promising to come again the next day. When he was gone I sat down to reflect more calmly. M. Leopold is a villain, that's clear, thought I. His designs regarding Ellen have been base, that's also clear. Have those designs been already accomplished? I must not believe it. Yet there was a dreadful sense of certainty in the surmise. Some one had whispered in my ear that morning that M. Leopold was going away—whispered, because there was little foundation for the report—and because (it was a shrewd guess for anybody to make) Ellen would be so disappointed. Pressure of business had kept the report out of my mind, until Morgan came. I would not tell him—no; he knew enough already. But now it was before me, and I felt sick at heart. If that were true, all was true! That must determine it. Yet we must not be idle. No, we would watch lynx-eyed. If not now too late, if not already gone down into that dread gulf which is fathomless, our kindly grasp would draw her from the brink. It seemed almost a vain hope, yet I encouraged it, and thus dismissed, or tried to, the harrowing theme.

The next morning, as I went early to my office, I

was painfully surprised to find Morgan standing at my door. Before I reached him I saw that something had transpired, for his face was pale and downcast. As I came up to him, he took my hand, and looked earnestly at me a moment, yet did not speak. We entered the office and sat down. For several minutes he remained silent, staring vacantly at the floor. I felt it was for him to speak first, and remained silent also. At last he said, mournfully:

"It seems strange to think what three days have brought to me—or, rather what they have taken from me. It seems like a dream. It must be a dream. I shall awake from it. I cannot live if I do not. How true was my instinct! I read it in her as well as in him. Must it be so? Dear, dear girl! It is an awful truth."

"What!" I exclaimed, torn with anguish. His face was ashy pale, and his eyes rolled fiercely.

"It is so," he resumed. "What a night I have passed! But away with these vain regrets. Blood is on the breeze—ay, blood! Life? Nonsense! Mr. D——, I have it to tell you. Last night that wretch was there—to see Ellen. I would not go into the room. I could not. I went early to my own room, which is directly over the parlor. For an hour or two it was quiet enough. Mother was gone to bed. Presently I heard a scornful laugh—the detestable voice! I knew it. 'I shall die'—in beseeching tones. It was Ellen. Another scornful laugh. 'Will you never come and see me?' she begged. 'Don't be foolish, girl.' Cold as an iceberg the tone was. Ellen was crying. I could hear her sob. 'Well, are you going to say good-by,' he went on in the same cold tone. 'How can you. Oh, my heart will break!' Such despair in her voice! I wanted to go down and cut *his* heart out; but I was chained to the spot. 'Don't make so much noise, you pretty wench, or I'll run now,' he said. 'Oh, I'll not speak. I never will speak again. But stay. Don't leave me.' She tried to talk low, but I heard distinctly. For a few moments neither of them said anything, or if they did, spoke in a whisper. 'Are you going,' she broke out almost in a shriek. 'Shut up. You'll raise the neighborhood. Let go of me! Come now. Now do be a quiet, staid, little maid, such as I *found* you, and let me go.' 'Tell me you will write to me. Tell me you will think of me. Oh, promise!' Such wild despair! 'Now, wench you're intolerable. Let me go. Do you hear? Let me go.' I heard a fall. The band was loosed. The next moment I was in the parlor.

He was gone, and Ellen lay there on the floor in a swoon. I called my mother, and we restored her, so that she could sit up; but her mind wandered. She could not collect her ideas so as to tell me where I would find the fiend, or she would not tell me, I don't know but that was it. She knows my temper. I did not trouble her much. I knew enough. The dreadful truth was clear. I believe my own mind wandered. For a moment it seemed he was before me. I clutched his heart and tore it from his body. I threw it upon the floor and stamped it. Mother led Ellen to her bed. Poor girl! She moaned. I never heard such a moan. It maddened me more than ever. But the phantasm was gone. All was reality! Oh, such a night as last night was! I could not think of sleep. But I'm calm now. About sunrise a strange calmness came over me,—so deep, so like a giant spirit breathing its whole energy into mine—that I was astonished. I feel it now."

I saw it in his face, and there was something awful about it, like the sense one gets from beholding a distant, steady gleam in the depths of night.

"There is one little hope," he resumed; "but I do not depend upon it. I don't know as I want to. Yet it shall be fairly done. Mr. D——, I have craved advice of you; but I don't ask it now. I don't want to implicate you. I only want you to go with me. I am young. I may not remain so calm; and want you to stand by me. I know you are my friend."

He reached out his hand, and I grasped it, returning his earnest look.

"Not a moment is to be lost now," he continued, rising, and we went out together. As we were walking along, he said, "You know his room; I will let you lead the way, if you please." The hotel was not far off, and we soon reached it. "Are you armed?" I asked, as we ascended the stairs.

"With truth and justice," he replied.

"Well, but that will not do," said I, halting. "You must have a more material weapon than those."

"I have thought it all over," he pursued, urging me forward. "I didn't know how the sight of him might madden me."

I could do no better than to yield, and we went on to M. Leopold's room.

The reception we met with was faultless in point of politeness. He was, apparently, in his happiest mood, and talked with us sometime upon miscellaneous, indifferent topics, with great vivacity and elogance of manner. Morgan sustained our part of the conversation. As for myself, I feared to open my mouth, lest I should betray my emotions. How Morgan kept so cool, I could not comprehend. His manner was light and easy, having nothing in it to betray, in the least, the object of his coming. While they were thus talking, I looked around the room. It gave evident signs of its tenant being about to depart Trunks, covered and strapped, ready for the porter; an overcoat and a cloak, carefully brushed, lying on the table, and a portmanteau by their side. There could be no mistake about it.

There was a pause of a minute or so in the conversation.

"You are about leaving, I see," said Morgan, as though it was a casual remark, looking around at the signs to which I have alluded.

"I am, sir," he replied, and there was a little defiance in the tone of his voice.

"When will you return, think you—if I may be so bold," Morgan inquired, as though it was nothing to him. I wondered more and more at his nonchalance

"It is doubtful, sir," replied M. Leopold, still somewhat defiant. I looked at Morgan. The veins of his neck and temples were full—the giant spirit was upon him. Bending slightly forward, and fixing his burning eyes upon M. Leopold, he said in a firm tone, "Do you know, sir, why I have come here this morning?"

M. Leopold was not surprised, nor apparently in the least disconcerted, and replied with a kind of mocking smile, "Well, indeed, I don't know, unless it was to bid me farewell. Our acquaintance is short, it is true, but"——

"Sir, you can dispense with that mockery," said Morgan, interrupting him. "I came here on more serious business than to bid you farewell. I came here, sir, in the first place, to ask you, and you must answer me, when you intend to return, or whether you intend to return at all or not."

"Yes, sir. Are you aware, my emblem of tender manhood, that you are decidedly impudent?"

"Answer me, sir, or the consequences be yours," said Morgan, rising to his feet.

"Aha! You think of forcing matters, I see. What do you think you will make out of it, eh?" Young man, sit down, and calmly hear me say that —are you going to stand? well, take it so, then— that, in short, sir, to come right to the point, for I'm getting serious, that I shall not probably visit your delightful town again—very soon. Now, sir,—I know it isn't polite, but circumstances demand it—will you leave this room?"

"No, sir, not till I have done. You acknowledge that you do not intend to return. I will spare you no longer. Base wretch!"—how scathingly he spoke it!—"you have done a deed which cannot be passed over. You are a villain. I beard you with the name! And I call heav"——

"Hold on, young man," hastily interrupted M. Leopold, with a low, husky voice—he had lost command of himself, and was pale with passion—"I'm not accustomed to this. Leave the room, or I'll fix you so that you can be carried out." He turned to his overcoat which was near at hand, and drew from one of the pockets a heavy pistol. Prompted by fear for my friend's life, I made a movement as though I would step between them; but Morgan held me back, saying in a manner that betokened the very opposite of fear, "He dare not shoot. Let us see if he dare;" and he raised himself to his fullest height, and, folding his arms, looked down contemptuously at M. Leopold. The latter clutched his weapon convulsively, and essayed to level it, but his hand trembled. After twice attempting, he desisted, and slowly arose to his feet.

"See the puppy!" Morgan exclaimed. "See the extent of his courage, will you? Oh! I want him to shoot me. He has stolen my life; I want him to take the semblance of it. Let"——

"Young man," interrupted M. Leopold with tolerable firmness of manner, though yet pale with the tumult of passion, "you have a commendable stock of bravery, I must confess—worthy of a better cause."

"A better cause!" exclaimed Morgan, with noble indignation.

"Yes, I mean it," resumed the other, growing calmer. "You are making a fine fool of yourself, without counting the cost. Moreover, I, for my part, can't see any *cause* about it; and I don't believe your friend here does, either. You come here and put impudent inquiries to me, and because I so deem them, you beard me with hard names. You must be laboring under some hallucination."

"Flimsy trash! You know what you have done. You know you deserve a lingering death at my hands. You know I would not descend to you, if you had not risen to pollute the fountain of my life. Vile wretch! Serpent! sneaking, detestable viper! I will curse you, and you shall hear me."

M. Leopold's anger again got the master of him.

"By G—d! I've a good mind to shoot him down," he said huskily, as though speaking to himself, glancing alternately at his weapon and at Morgan.

"Shoot, villain!" said Morgan, with a sublime defiance; "I shall have a dying word for you, that will gore your black heart for ever."

M. Leopold did not seem to have heard the remark, but went on speaking to himself. "No, I have had enough of it. Pshaw! and all this for a girl! Young man," he continued, looking at Morgan, "you had better go home, and say nothing about it. I left the girl as I *found* her, do you understand?"

Like a thunderbolt, and as quick, a heavy blow laid him senseless upon the floor. It was Morgan did it, exclaiming, "Swallow your foul words! I can no longer forbear." Then turning to me he said calmly, "If I have killed him, think you I have not done right?"

I stooped to examine the insensible man. He was not dead. In a few moments he opened his eyes, and with much effort raised himself upon his elbow. As soon as he had recovered his voice, he said, "Young man, this act demands satisfaction. You will hear from me soon. I hope you will not refuse."

Morgan made no reply, but turning slowly, as though impelled, left the room. I followed him, and we went back to the office.

"It looks," said Morgan, after we had sat a few minutes in silence, "as though I went there on purpose to provoke him to a duel, don't it? But that was not my intention. I only wanted to-day to have him hear me curse him—curse him as his damning crime deserves. I did not say half I meant to. His imputation overcame my prudence. If that blow had killed him I should have been sorry, for I know that a few years, if he live, will bring remorse—a punishment more terrible than man can invent. Do you think he will challenge me?"

I could see no reason to doubt it, and told him so.

"It is not that I shrink from death; but Ellen would have no friend to protect her if I should fall, and I do not want to kill him *so*; vengeance would be half cheated of its prey if I should. I hope he will not challenge me."

After about an hour, Morgan went away. It was Thursday this happened—Saturday I saw him again. He had received a challenge, and accepted it, and came to ask me if I would serve as his assistant. At first I thought I would decline, but I felt that the die was cast, that the dreadful test was inevitable, and I ought not—I could not, the more I thought of it—forsake him. When I had acceded to his desire, we went out and walked together. He talked of Ellen. "Poor girl!" he exclaimed, "she grows worse and worse. She moans and weeps continually. She will not eat, and she sleeps scarcely at all. She will answer questions, seems to comprehend what is going on about her, yet pays little attention to it. Her bodily strength is rapidly failing. I am afraid she will die. She thinks the villain is gone. She knows nothing about what is brewing. I don't want her to, until the result be known. She loves the beastly scoundrel. Oh, what infatuation! I'm going to kill him if I can do it fairly; and if I do, I suppose she will hate me for it—if she live. But she will not live. Her heart is broken. I know it."

We walked on, and came back to my office. Just before we separated, he took my hand, saying, "Mr. D——, I don't feel just as I did the other day, about that wretch. I have come to the conclusion that he deserves immediate death—that he ought not to roam farther on his desolating course. I do not mean to assassinate him. But in the coming contest, you must not look for compromise. One of us *must* die. If he live at the expense of my life, perhaps remorse will visit him earlier. At all events I shall have done my duty."

The preliminaries were arranged. The meeting was to take place on the following Monday afternoon in a secluded spot—a kind of glade—some three miles from town. The weapons were to be pistols, and the distance ten paces.

During the intervening Sunday, I was with Morgan. For an hour or two towards evening I was at his mother's. Oh, what a change since I had been there!—an interval of one week. Ellen, the brilliant, the beautiful, the hopeful——a wreck. Pale and haggard, her eyes almost blind with weeping, her once glossy tresses wildly scattered over her stooping form, she walked to and fro in her room, moaning unceasingly.

"I love them, but they don't love me,"—the distant recollection came, and I wept unreservedly. I did not seek to disturb her, but tearfully contemplated her through the open door of her room, until, becoming aware of my presence, she shut herself from my sight. The mother, bowed with extremest sorrow, sat in silence, as one bereaved of all that could sweeten life. The brother—what a change in him! In his youth, in his day of most glorious hope, a viper had stung him, and turned all to darkness. There was life yet—fierce, pent energy, which must work out in its terrible power, before the wreck should be complete.

It was too mournful. I could not bear it, and hurried away.

Early in the afternoon, Monday, Morgan came to the hotel, where I had promised to be, and we repaired to the place of meeting. We were first on the ground, and sat down at the base of an old tree to await the coming of the others. It was October. The autumn frosts had done more than half their work. Tall trees had begun to show their boughs bleakly against the sky, and embowered vistas were coming to be naked, desolate paths. A blue mist hovered upon the distant hills, resting less dense upon the broad plain that intervened. The mist was quiet—silent. The sunlight, too, was quiet, and the winds, yet eloquent all—their voice the rustling of the falling leaves. The great Anthem of the Year was in its minor key, and one note bore the burden of the melting strain.

"Talk to me, Mr. D——, I am very wretched," said Morgan.

"What shall it be about?" I asked, counterfeiting an encouraging smile.

"Oh, I don't know," he replied, sinking back; "only it seems I shall go wild. I don't want you to say anything. Did it ever seem so quiet and mournful before? Oh, so mournful! Dear, dear Ellen! My sister. What has been done? We used to come here together for berries and autumn-flowers—years ago. She is not dead. Why not blot out this awful thing, and be as we were once, again? Alas! it is a fixed reality. Death alone can change it. It will be changed soon. Her days are numbered. When she shall be in the grave, if I live, I may feel a melancholy satisfaction—I may at least come to recall these awful days, and not be overwhelmed. Hark! did I hear a voice? Yes, there they come."

We stood up, and they came towards us. M. Leopold and his assistant on foot, having left their carriage a short distance away. M. Leopold was dressed in a complete suit of grey, and walked with his eyes cast down and his hands behind him. They halted a few rods from us, and his second beckoning, I went towards them. The solemn preliminaries were soon arranged, and the combatants took the positions assigned them. When I placed the weapon of death in Morgan's hand, he said with a firm, yet mournful voice:

"You know what to say to mother and Ellen if I fall. Break the truth carefully to them, but tell them the truth." He then added in a whisper, "Watch keenly. There'll be foul play, I fear. I see he has a knife. Don't let him get to me."

"Are you ready?" inquired M. Leopold's assistant of the antagonists. They assented. The word was given. A few moments—awful, insupportably awful, and the rigid grasp of suspense was broken by the sharp, thrilling reports—an instant apart.

"Are you hurt?" I asked rushing up to Morgan.

"No," he responded, smiling scornfully at his antagonist; "but *he* is hurt!"

I turned quickly, and saw M. Leopold struggling in the grasp of his assistant.

"Let me go!" he howled, in wild frenzy. "Let me go! Let me reach him. Get out my knife for me. I swear I can't see. O, God!—too deep!—Oh! Oh!" and with a ghastly shudder he sank lifeless.

I assisted in bearing the remains to the carriage. When we had adjusted them, and the man had mounted to his seat, I looked around for Morgan. He was gone. I lingered about for a while waiting; but he did not make his appearance; and, at length I returned to town, going to my office as though nothing had happened.

They bore the tidings to Ellen. At first she would not believe them; but being solemnly assured, the anguishing truth came to her shattered mind.

"He is dead, and my brother killed him," she said tremblingly, and with a low, desolate wail, she sank insensible.

Unhappy being! From that hour she was dead tc this world. A slow, consuming fever, accompanied with stupor and delirium, took fatal hold upon her, and day by day the lingering traces of what she once was passed away.

At length her physician announced that she must die. We gathered around her couch. It was night. She murmured in her delirium, and we bent to catch the sounds. "Brother, brother," wildly pathetic. A shadow darkened the wall, and suddenly a tall form stood by the bed. It was Morgan, unexpectedly returned.

"Ellen," said he appealingly, taking her passive hand, "Ellen, do you know me? I am Morgan."

She stared vacantly at him, and then closed her eyes. She did not know him. He bent closer and kissed her. Then, quivering with a grief that has no tears, he left the room. Again we heard her murmur "Brother;" but we knew it was only a wandering memory of other years, and we did not call him back.

Her breath grew fainter, fainter. We gazed in silence, broken only by the sobs of the agonized mother. As we gazed a sudden light gleamed from the eyes of the dying one. She raised her hands as if reaching for some treasure almost within her grasp, and that magic smile shot forth its thrilling radiance. She seemed about to speak, but with a long sigh she ceased to breathe. The light of her eyes was gone; the smile became as a smile in marble. Ellen's spirit was no longer ours to know and love.

Thus the sorrowful remembrance which thirty-five years had scarcely dimmed, came to me, and I wept afresh, and turning from the hallowed grave, I went away sated with sadness.

THE END.

www.ingramcontent.com/pod-product-compliance
Lightning Source LLC
LaVergne TN
LVHW010150110826
845151LV00002B/479

9781425536886